TEACHER'S PET PUBLICATIONS

PUZZLE PACK
for
Freak the Mighty

based on the book by
Rodman Philbrick

Written by
Mary B. Collins and Stacy C. Littleton

© 2007 Teacher's Pet Publications
All Rights Reserved

The materials in this packet are copyrighted
by Teacher's Pet Publications, Inc.

These pages may be duplicated by the purchaser
for use in the purchaser's own classroom.

Copying any of these materials and distributing them
for any other purpose is a violation of the copyright laws.

© 2007 Teacher's Pet Publications, Inc.
www.tpet.com

INTRODUCTION
If you already own the LitPlan for this title, this Puzzle Pack will refresh your Unit Resource Materials and Vocabulary Resource Materials sections plus give you additional materials you can substitute into the tests. If you do not already have a complete LitPlan, these pages will give you some supplemental materials to use with your own plan. There are two main groups of materials: one set for unit words (such as characters' names, symbols, places, etc.) and one set for vocabulary words associated with the book.

WORD LIST
There is a word list for both the unit words and the vocabulary words. These lists show you which words are being used in the materials and the clues or definitions being used for those words. You may want to give students a word list with clues/definitions to help them, or you may want students to only have a word list (without clues/definitions) if you want them to work a little harder. Both are available for duplication. The word lists can also be your "calling key" for the bingo games.

FILL IN THE BLANK AND MATCHING
There are 4 each of the fill in the blank and matching worksheets for both the unit and vocabulary words. These pages can be used either as extra worksheets for students or as objective parts of a unit test. They can be done individually if students need extra help or as a whole class activity to review the material covered.

MAGIC SQUARES
The magic squares not only reinforce the material covered but also work on reasoning and math skills. Many teachers have told us that their students really enjoy doing these!

WORD SEARCH PUZZLES
The word search words go in all directions, as indicated on your answer keys. Two of the word search puzzles have the clues listed rather than the words. This makes the puzzle a little more difficult, but it reinforces the material better. Two word search puzzles have words only for students who find the clue puzzles too difficult.

CROSSWORD PUZZLES
Both unit and vocabulary word sections have 4 crossword puzzles.

BINGO CARDS
There are 32 individual bingo cards for the unit words and 32 individual bingo cards for the vocabulary words. You can use your word list as a "call list," calling the words at random and marking them off of your list as you go, or you could use the flash cards by cutting them apart and drawing the words at random from a hat (or box or whatever). To make a better review, you might ask for the definition and spelling of each word as you call it out–or you could call out the definitions and have students tell you the words they need to look for on the puzzle.

JUGGLE LETTERS
The vocabulary juggle letter game is intended to help students learn the spellings of the words. One sheet has the definitions listed on it as an extra help for students who need it or to reinforce the definitions if you choose to do so.

FLASH CARDS
We've included a set of vocabulary flash cards you can duplicate, cut, and fold for your students. Some teachers make a few sets for general use by the class; others make a set for each student. Some teachers duplicate them for each student and have the students cut & fold their own. You can cut out just the words and put them in a hat, have each student pick out one word and write the definition and a sentence for that word. Students then swap words and papers, with the next student adding a sentence of his own under the last one. You can have students swap as many times as you like. Each time the student will read the sentences written prior to his own and then add a sentence. You can cut out the words and definitions separately and play "I Have; Who Has?" Each student in the room draws a word and definition. The first student says, "I have (the name of the word). Who has the definition?" The student with the definition reads it then says, "I have (the name of the vocabulary word she has). Who has the definition?" The round continues until all words and definitions have been given.

Freak the Mighty Word List

No.	Word	Clue/Definition
1.	ADDISON	Principal
2.	ARTHUR	King ____, once a wimpy little kid, an orphan who pulled a sword from the stone
3.	BIONIC	The Experimental ____ Unit: where Freak will become the first bionically improved human
4.	BLADE	Tony D's nickname
5.	BOOK	Freak gives Max a blank one and tells him to fill it with their adventures.
6.	BRAIN	What Max didn't have until Freak came along
7.	CHARACTER	Grim is concerned Max will inherit this from his father.
8.	COMICS	Kevin wrapped Max's Christmas present with this
9.	CRETIN	What Freak calls Tony D
10.	DICTIONARY	Freak writes one for Max.
11.	DONELLI	Sends Max and Freak to the principal's office
12.	EXCALIBUR	King Arthur's magical sword
13.	FLOATING	How Max feels when he goes to the place in his head
14.	FLOUR	Max at first only knows King Arthur as the brand of ____ Gram uses.
15.	FREAK	He talks like a dictionary and sits on Max's shoulders.
16.	GRAM	Max's grandmother
17.	GRIM	He built the Down Under.
18.	GUILTY	Killer Kane's plea before going to trial
19.	GUINEVERE	One of the names Kevin uses for his mother
20.	GWEN	Friend of Max's mother
21.	HERO	What the police call Max for saving Kevin
22.	HIM	Max's father
23.	ICU	Where Freak dies
24.	IGGY	Boss of the Panheads
25.	INSIDE	Freak grew on the ____ but not on the outside.
26.	KANE	Killer ____; Max's father
27.	KNIGHTS	First human version of robots, according to Freak
28.	LIFE	____ is dangerous.
29.	LORETTA	Heroic Biker Babe
30.	MAX	The Mighty part of Freak the Mighty
31.	MILLPOND	Where Freak the Mighty is born
32.	ORNITHOPTER	Plastic bird
33.	PAIN	According to Freak, it is just a state of mind.
34.	PAROLE	Killer Kane violated his ____.
35.	PHILBRICK	Author of Freak the Mighty
36.	PREACHER	Killer Kane planned to become one to get money.
37.	PURSE	The object of the treasure hunt
38.	PYRAMID	Max's Christmas present from Freak is in a box shaped like a ____.
39.	READ	Freak taught Max how to do this better.
40.	REMEMBERING	____ is just an invention of the mind.
41.	SEIZURE	What happens to Freak on his birthday
42.	SHOULDERS	Freak sits on Max's ____.
43.	SPIVAK	Kevin's doctor
44.	STRANGLE	Killer Kane's method of killing
45.	SULFURIC	Freaks sprays Killer Kane in the eyes with fake ____ acid.
46.	TESTAMENTS	Loretta and Iggy live in the New ____.
47.	WHISTLES	How Freak gets the cops' attention
48.	WRITING	It is like talking, according to Max

Freak the Mighty Fill In The Blanks 1

1. Max at first only knows King Arthur as the brand of ____ Gram uses.
2. The Experimental ____ Unit: where Freak will become the first bionically improved human
3. Freak writes one for Max.
4. What the police call Max for saving Kevin
5. Kevin wrapped Max's Christmas present with this.
6. Killer ____; Max's father
7. Freak sprays Killer Kane in the eyes with fake ____ acid.
8. Tony D's nickname
9. Killer Kane violated his ___.
10. How Max feels when he goes to the place in his head
11. Max's grandmother
12. Author of Freak the Mighty
13. King ____; once a wimpy little kid, an orphan who pulled a sword from the stone
14. Freak grew on the ____ but not on the outside.
15. One of the names Kevin uses for his mother
16. What Max didn't have until Freak came along
17. Max's father
18. Freak sits on Max's ___.
19. Where Freak the Mighty is born
20. Plastic bird

Freak the Mighty Fill In The Blanks 1 Answer Key

FLOUR	1. Max at first only knows King Arthur as the brand of ____ Gram uses.
BIONIC	2. The Experimental ____ Unit: where Freak will become the first bionically improved human
DICTIONARY	3. Freak writes one for Max.
HERO	4. What the police call Max for saving Kevin
COMICS	5. Kevin wrapped Max's Christmas present with this
KANE	6. Killer ____; Max's father
SULFURIC	7. Freak sprays Killer Kane in the eyes with fake ____ acid.
BLADE	8. Tony D's nickname
PAROLE	9. Killer Kane violated his ___.
FLOATING	10. How Max feels when he goes to the place in his head
GRAM	11. Max's grandmother
PHILBRICK	12. Author of Freak the Mighty
ARTHUR	13. King ____; once a wimpy little kid, an orphan who pulled a sword from the stone
INSIDE	14. Freak grew on the ____ but not on the outside.
GUINEVERE	15. One of the names Kevin uses for his mother
BRAIN	16. What Max didn't have until Freak came along
HIM	17. Max's father
SHOULDERS	18. Freak sits on Max's ___.
MILLPOND	19. Where Freak the Mighty is born
ORNITHOPTER	20. Plastic bird

Freak the Mighty Fill In The Blanks 2

_____ 1. What Max didn't have until Freak came along

_____ 2. What happens to Freak on his birthday

_____ 3. Freak gives Max a blank one and tells him to fill it with their adventures.

_____ 4. Heroic Biker Babe

_____ 5. Killer Kane planned to become one to get money.

_____ 6. The object of the treasure hunt

_____ 7. What Freak calls Tony D

_____ 8. Max's Christmas present from Freak is in a box shaped like a ____.

_____ 9. Loretta and Iggy live in the New ____.

_____ 10. Max's father

_____ 11. How Freak gets the cops' attention

_____ 12. Where Freak dies

_____ 13. ____ is just an invention of the mind.

_____ 14. Freak sits on Max's ___.

_____ 15. First human version of robots, according to Freak

_____ 16. Where Freak the Mighty is born

_____ 17. Freak writes one for Max.

_____ 18. Kevin wrapped Max's Christmas present with this.

_____ 19. Tony D's nickname

_____ 20. Sends Max and Freak to the principal's office

Freak the Mighty Fill In The Blanks 2 Answer Key

BRAIN	1. What Max didn't have until Freak came along
SEIZURE	2. What happens to Freak on his birthday
BOOK	3. Freak gives Max a blank one and tells him to fill it with their adventures.
LORETTA	4. Heroic Biker Babe
PREACHER	5. Killer Kane planned to become one to get money.
PURSE	6. The object of the treasure hunt
CRETIN	7. What Freak calls Tony D
PYRAMID	8. Max's Christmas present from Freak is in a box shaped like a ____.
TESTAMENTS	9. Loretta and Iggy live in the New ____.
HIM	10. Max's father
WHISTLES	11. How Freak gets the cops' attention
ICU	12. Where Freak dies
REMEMBERING	13. ____ is just an invention of the mind.
SHOULDERS	14. Freak sits on Max's ___.
KNIGHTS	15. First human version of robots, according to Freak
MILLPOND	16. Where Freak the Mighty is born
DICTIONARY	17. Freak writes one for Max.
COMICS	18. Kevin wrapped Max's Christmas present with this.
BLADE	19. Tony D's nickname
DONELLI	20. Sends Max and Freak to the principal's office

Freak the Mighty Fill In The Blanks 3

_____

1. Where Freak the Mighty is born
2. Max's grandmother
3. Killer ____; Max's father
4. Freak writes one for Max.
5. Killer Kane violated his ___.
6. He talks like a dictionary and sits on Max's shoulders.
7. Freak sprays Killer Kane in the eyes with fake ____ acid.
8. What Freak calls Tony D
9. ____ is just an invention of the mind.
10. What happens to Freak on his birthday
11. What the police call Max for saving Kevin
12. According to Freak, it is just a state of mind.
13. King Arthur's magical sword
14. Killer Kane planned to become one to get money.
15. Author of Freak the Mighty
16. Loretta and Iggy live in the New ____.
17. He built the Down Under.
18. Where Freak dies
19. Boss of the Panheads
20. King ____; once a wimpy little kid, an orphan who pulled a sword from the stone

Freak the Mighty Fill In The Blanks 3 Answer Key

MILLPOND	1. Where Freak the Mighty is born
GRAM	2. Max's grandmother
KANE	3. Killer ____; Max's father
DICTIONARY	4. Freak writes one for Max.
PAROLE	5. Killer Kane violated his ___.
FREAK	6. He talks like a dictionary and sits on Max's shoulders.
SULFURIC	7. Freak sprays Killer Kane in the eyes with fake ____ acid.
CRETIN	8. What Freak calls Tony D
REMEMBERING	9. ____ is just an invention of the mind.
SEIZURE	10. What happens to Freak on his birthday
HERO	11. What the police call Max for saving Kevin
PAIN	12. According to Freak, it is just a state of mind.
EXCALIBUR	13. King Arthur's magical sword
PREACHER	14. Killer Kane planned to become one to get money.
PHILBRICK	15. Author of Freak the Mighty
TESTAMENTS	16. Loretta and Iggy live in the New ____.
GRIM	17. He built the Down Under.
ICU	18. Where Freak dies
IGGY	19. Boss of the Panheads
ARTHUR	20. King ____; once a wimpy little kid, an orphan who pulled a sword from the stone

Freak the Mighty Fill In The Blanks 4

_____   1. Friend of Max's mother

_____   2. Sends Max and Freak to the principal's office

_____   3. The Experimental ____ Unit: where Freak will become the first bionically improved human

_____   4. Killer Kane's method of killing

_____   5. What Max didn't have until Freak came along

_____   6. Heroic Biker Babe

_____   7. What Freak calls Tony D

_____   8. How Freak gets the cops' attention

_____   9. He talks like a dictionary and sits on Max's shoulders.

_____   10. Killer Kane's plea before going to trial

_____   11. Killer ____; Max's father

_____   12. One of the names Kevin uses for his mother

_____   13. The object of the treasure hunt

_____   14. What the police call Max for saving Kevin

_____   15. Freak gives Max a blank one and tells him to fill it with their adventures.

_____   16. He built the Down Under.

_____   17. Freak writes one for Max.

_____   18. Where Freak the Mighty is born

_____   19. Tony D's nickname

_____   20. Max's grandmother

Freak the Mighty Fill In The Blanks 4 Answer Key

GWEN	1. Friend of Max's mother
DONELLI	2. Sends Max and Freak to the principal's office
BIONIC	3. The Experimental ____ Unit: where Freak will become the first bionically improved human
STRANGLE	4. Killer Kane's method of killing
BRAIN	5. What Max didn't have until Freak came along
LORETTA	6. Heroic Biker Babe
CRETIN	7. What Freak calls Tony D
WHISTLES	8. How Freak gets the cops' attention
FREAK	9. He talks like a dictionary and sits on Max's shoulders.
GUILTY	10. Killer Kane's plea before going to trial
KANE	11. Killer ____; Max's father
GUINEVERE	12. One of the names Kevin uses for his mother
PURSE	13. The object of the treasure hunt
HERO	14. What the police call Max for saving Kevin
BOOK	15. Freak gives Max a blank one and tells him to fill it with their adventures.
GRIM	16. He built the Down Under.
DICTIONARY	17. Freak writes one for Max
MILLPOND	18. Where Freak the Mighty is born
BLADE	19. Tony D's nickname
GRAM	20. Max's grandmother

Freak the Mighty Matching 1

___ 1. PURSE   A. First human version of robots, according to Freak
___ 2. KNIGHTS   B. Freak gives Max a blank one and tells him to fill it with their adventures.
___ 3. GUINEVERE   C. What happens to Freak on his birthday
___ 4. CHARACTER   D. What Max didn't have until Freak came along
___ 5. BOOK   E. Where Freak the Mighty is born
___ 6. GWEN   F. Grim is concerned Max will inherit this from his father.
___ 7. DONELLI   G. What the police call Max for saving Kevin
___ 8. BRAIN   H. ____ is just an invention of the mind.
___ 9. SEIZURE   I. Freak sits on Max's ___.
___10. LORETTA   J. Killer ____; Max's father
___11. MAX   K. Freak writes one for Max.
___12. EXCALIBUR   L. Where Freak dies
___13. KANE   M. Freak sprays Killer Kane in the eyes with fake ____ acid.
___14. SPIVAK   N. One of the names Kevin uses for his mother
___15. MILLPOND   O. The object of the treasure hunt
___16. PYRAMID   P. According to Freak, it is just a state of mind.
___17. FREAK   Q. Friend of Max's mother
___18. SHOULDERS   R. Heroic Biker Babe
___19. ORNITHOPTER   S. Plastic bird
___20. PAIN   T. Sends Max and Freak to the principal's office
___21. DICTIONARY   U. He talks like a dictionary and sits on Max's shoulders.
___22. ICU   V. Max's Christmas present from Freak is in a box shaped like a ____.
___23. REMEMBERING   W. King Arthur's magical sword
___24. HERO   X. Kevin's doctor
___25. SULFURIC   Y. The Mighty part of Freak the Mighty

Freak the Mighty Matching 1 Answer Key

O - 1. PURSE	A.	First human version of robots, according to Freak
A - 2. KNIGHTS	B.	Freak gives Max a blank one and tells him to fill it with their adventures.
N - 3. GUINEVERE	C.	What happens to Freak on his birthday
F - 4. CHARACTER	D.	What Max didn't have until Freak came along
B - 5. BOOK	E.	Where Freak the Mighty is born
Q - 6. GWEN	F.	Grim is concerned Max will inherit this from his father.
T - 7. DONELLI	G.	What the police call Max for saving Kevin
D - 8. BRAIN	H.	____ is just an invention of the mind.
C - 9. SEIZURE	I.	Freak sits on Max's ___.
R - 10. LORETTA	J.	Killer ____; Max's father
Y - 11. MAX	K.	Freak writes one for Max.
W - 12. EXCALIBUR	L.	Where Freak dies
J - 13. KANE	M.	Freak sprays Killer Kane in the eyes with fake ____ acid.
X - 14. SPIVAK	N.	One of the names Kevin uses for his mother
E - 15. MILLPOND	O.	The object of the treasure hunt
V - 16. PYRAMID	P.	According to Freak, it is just a state of mind.
U - 17. FREAK	Q.	Friend of Max's mother
I - 18. SHOULDERS	R.	Heroic Biker Babe
S - 19. ORNITHOPTER	S.	Plastic bird
P - 20. PAIN	T.	Sends Max and Freak to the principal's office
K - 21. DICTIONARY	U.	He talks like a dictionary and sits on Max's shoulders.
L - 22. ICU	V.	Max's Christmas present from Freak is in a box shaped like a ____.
H - 23. REMEMBERING	W.	King Arthur's magical sword
G - 24. HERO	X.	Kevin's doctor
M - 25. SULFURIC	Y.	The Mighty part of Freak the Mighty

Freak the Mighty Matching 2

___ 1. HIM
___ 2. CRETIN
___ 3. SHOULDERS
___ 4. PHILBRICK
___ 5. EXCALIBUR
___ 6. DONELLI
___ 7. ICU
___ 8. WRITING
___ 9. INSIDE
___ 10. BIONIC
___ 11. GUILTY
___ 12. BRAIN
___ 13. CHARACTER
___ 14. FLOUR
___ 15. PYRAMID
___ 16. BOOK
___ 17. PAIN
___ 18. ORNITHOPTER
___ 19. LORETTA
___ 20. BLADE
___ 21. TESTAMENTS
___ 22. PREACHER
___ 23. GRAM
___ 24. GRIM
___ 25. LIFE

A. King Arthur's magical sword
B. What Freak calls Tony D
C. He built the Down Under.
D. What Max didn't have until Freak came along
E. Max's Christmas present from Freak is in a box shaped like a ____.
F. Freak sits on Max's ___.
G. Where Freak dies
H. Max's father
I. According to Freak, it is just a state of mind.
J. Max's grandmother
K. It is like talking, according to Max.
L. Max at first only knows King Arthur as the brand of ____ Gram uses.
M. The Experimental ____ Unit: where Freak will become the first bionically improved human
N. Author of Freak the Mighty
O. Freak gives Max a blank one and tells him to fill it with their adventures.
P. Sends Max and Freak to the principal's office
Q. ____ is dangerous.
R. Tony D's nickname
S. Heroic Biker Babe
T. Killer Kane planned to become one to get money.
U. Loretta and Iggy live in the New ____.
V. Killer Kane's plea before going to trial
W. Grim is concerned Max will inherit this from his father.
X. Freak grew on the ____ but not on the outside.
Y. Plastic bird

Freak the Mighty Matching 2 Answer Key

H - 1. HIM
B - 2. CRETIN
F - 3. SHOULDERS
N - 4. PHILBRICK
A - 5. EXCALIBUR
P - 6. DONELLI
G - 7. ICU
K - 8. WRITING
X - 9. INSIDE
M - 10. BIONIC
V - 11. GUILTY
D - 12. BRAIN
W - 13. CHARACTER
L - 14. FLOUR
E - 15. PYRAMID
O - 16. BOOK
I - 17. PAIN
Y - 18. ORNITHOPTER
S - 19. LORETTA
R - 20. BLADE
U - 21. TESTAMENTS
T - 22. PREACHER
J - 23. GRAM
C - 24. GRIM
Q - 25. LIFE

A. King Arthur's magical sword
B. What Freak calls Tony D
C. He built the Down Under.
D. What Max didn't have until Freak came along
E. Max's Christmas present from Freak is in a box shaped like a ____.
F. Freak sits on Max's ___.
G. Where Freak dies
H. Max's father
I. According to Freak, it is just a state of mind.
J. Max's grandmother
K. It is like talking, according to Max.
L. Max at first only knows King Arthur as the brand of ____ Gram uses.
M. The Experimental ____ Unit: where Freak will become the first bionically improved human
N. Author of Freak the Mighty
O. Freak gives Max a blank one and tells him to fill it with their adventures.
P. Sends Max and Freak to the principal's office
Q. ____ is dangerous.
R. Tony D's nickname
S. Heroic Biker Babe
T. Killer Kane planned to become one to get money.
U. Loretta and Iggy live in the New ____.
V. Killer Kane's plea before going to trial
W. Grim is concerned Max will inherit this from his father.
X. Freak grew on the ____ but not on the outside.
Y. Plastic bird

Freak the Mighty Matching 3

___ 1. BLADE   A. Grim is concerned Max will inherit this from his father.
___ 2. LORETTA   B. The Experimental ____ Unit: where Freak will become the first bionically improved human
___ 3. PURSE   C. He built the Down Under.
___ 4. GRAM   D. Plastic bird
___ 5. KANE   E. Kevin wrapped Max's Christmas present with this.
___ 6. DONELLI   F. King Arthur's magical sword
___ 7. GUINEVERE   G. Max's father
___ 8. PREACHER   H. It is like talking, according to Max.
___ 9. INSIDE   I. Sends Max and Freak to the principal's office
___ 10. COMICS   J. He talks like a dictionary and sits on Max's shoulders.
___ 11. ADDISON   K. First human version of robots, according to Freak
___ 12. EXCALIBUR   L. The object of the treasure hunt
___ 13. GRIM   M. Principal
___ 14. STRANGLE   N. Friend of Max's mother
___ 15. ORNITHOPTER   O. Killer Kane's method of killing
___ 16. BIONIC   P. Heroic Biker Babe
___ 17. HIM   Q. One of the names Kevin uses for his mother
___ 18. MAX   R. Max's grandmother
___ 19. TESTAMENTS   S. Freak grew on the ____ but not on the outside.
___ 20. GWEN   T. Loretta and Iggy live in the New ____.
___ 21. WRITING   U. Killer ____; Max's father
___ 22. KNIGHTS   V. What the police call Max for saving Kevin
___ 23. FREAK   W. Killer Kane planned to become one to get money.
___ 24. CHARACTER   X. The Mighty part of Freak the Mighty
___ 25. HERO   Y. Tony D's nickname

Freak the Mighty Matching 3 Answer Key

Y - 1. BLADE		A. Grim is concerned Max will inherit this from his father.
P - 2. LORETTA		B. The Experimental ____ Unit: where Freak will become the first bionically improved human
L - 3. PURSE		C. He built the Down Under.
R - 4. GRAM		D. Plastic bird
U - 5. KANE		E. Kevin wrapped Max's Christmas present with this.
I - 6. DONELLI		F. King Arthur's magical sword
Q - 7. GUINEVERE		G. Max's father
W - 8. PREACHER		H. It is like talking, according to Max.
S - 9. INSIDE		I. Sends Max and Freak to the principal's office
E - 10. COMICS		J. He talks like a dictionary and sits on Max's shoulders.
M - 11. ADDISON		K. First human version of robots, according to Freak
F - 12. EXCALIBUR		L. The object of the treasure hunt
C - 13. GRIM		M. Principal
O - 14. STRANGLE		N. Friend of Max's mother
D - 15. ORNITHOPTER		O. Killer Kane's method of killing
B - 16. BIONIC		P. Heroic Biker Babe
G - 17. HIM		Q. One of the names Kevin uses for his mother
X - 18. MAX		R. Max's grandmother
T - 19. TESTAMENTS		S. Freak grew on the ____ but not on the outside.
N - 20. GWEN		T. Loretta and Iggy live in the New ____.
H - 21. WRITING		U. Killer ____; Max's father
K - 22. KNIGHTS		V. What the police call Max for saving Kevin
J - 23. FREAK		W. Killer Kane planned to become one to get money.
A - 24. CHARACTER		X. The Mighty part of Freak the Mighty
V - 25. HERO		Y. Tony D's nickname

Freak the Mighty Matching 4

___ 1. ORNITHOPTER   A. What happens to Freak on his birthday
___ 2. GRAM   B. What the police call Max for saving Kevin
___ 3. BOOK   C. Heroic Biker Babe
___ 4. SEIZURE   D. Killer Kane's method of killing
___ 5. ARTHUR   E. Freak taught Max how to do this better.
___ 6. COMICS   F. Freak gives Max a blank one and tells him to fill it with their adventures.
___ 7. KNIGHTS   G. Max's grandmother
___ 8. CRETIN   H. ____ is dangerous.
___ 9. LIFE   I. Killer ____; Max's father
___10. DICTIONARY   J. He built the Down Under.
___11. TESTAMENTS   K. Tony D's nickname
___12. BLADE   L. Max's Christmas present from Freak is in a box shaped like a ____.
___13. STRANGLE   M. Loretta and Iggy live in the New ____.
___14. READ   N. Principal
___15. KANE   O. First human version of robots, according to Freak
___16. PURSE   P. Max at first only knows King Arthur as the brand of ____ Gram uses.
___17. LORETTA   Q. King ____; once a wimpy little kid, an orphan who pulled a sword from the stone
___18. ADDISON   R. Killer Kane's plea before going to trial
___19. GUILTY   S. Kevin wrapped Max's Christmas present with this.
___20. GRIM   T. Boss of the Panheads
___21. ICU   U. The object of the treasure hunt
___22. IGGY   V. Plastic bird
___23. FLOUR   W. What Freak calls Tony D
___24. PYRAMID   X. Freak writes one for Max.
___25. HERO   Y. Where Freak dies

Freak the Mighty Matching 4 Answer Key

V - 1. ORNITHOPTER		A. What happens to Freak on his birthday
G - 2. GRAM		B. What the police call Max for saving Kevin
F - 3. BOOK		C. Heroic Biker Babe
A - 4. SEIZURE		D. Killer Kane's method of killing
Q - 5. ARTHUR		E. Freak taught Max how to do this better.
S - 6. COMICS		F. Freak gives Max a blank one and tells him to fill it with their adventures.
O - 7. KNIGHTS		G. Max's grandmother
W - 8. CRETIN		H. ____ is dangerous.
H - 9. LIFE		I. Killer ____; Max's father
X - 10. DICTIONARY		J. He built the Down Under.
M - 11. TESTAMENTS		K. Tony D's nickname
K - 12. BLADE		L. Max's Christmas present from Freak is in a box shaped like a ____.
D - 13. STRANGLE		M. Loretta and Iggy live in the New ____.
E - 14. READ		N. Principal
I - 15. KANE		O. First human version of robots, according to Freak
U - 16. PURSE		P. Max at first only knows King Arthur as the brand of ____ Gram uses.
C - 17. LORETTA		Q. King ____; once a wimpy little kid, an orphan who pulled a sword from the stone
N - 18. ADDISON		R. Killer Kane's plea before going to trial
R - 19. GUILTY		S. Kevin wrapped Max's Christmas present with this.
J - 20. GRIM		T. Boss of the Panheads
Y - 21. ICU		U. The object of the treasure hunt
T - 22. IGGY		V. Plastic bird
P - 23. FLOUR		W. What Freak calls Tony D
L - 24. PYRAMID		X. Freak writes one for Max.
B - 25. HERO		Y. Where Freak dies

Freak the Mighty Magic Squares 1

Match the definition with the vocabulary word. Put your answers in the magic squares below. When your answers are correct, all columns and rows will add to the same number.

A. SHOULDERS
B. BRAIN
C. STRANGLE
D. DONELLI
E. PREACHER
F. GUINEVERE
G. LORETTA
H. COMICS
I. PURSE
J. LIFE
K. ADDISON
L. FLOATING
M. ARTHUR
N. CHARACTER
O. GUILTY
P. BOOK

1. King ____; once a wimpy little kid, an orphan who pulled a sword from the stone
2. One of the names Kevin uses for his mother
3. Kevin wrapped Max's Christmas present with this.
4. Killer Kane's plea before going to trial
5. How Max feels when he goes to the place in his head
6. Killer Kane's method of killing
7. Freak sits on Max's ___.
8. ____ is dangerous.
9. Principal
10. Sends Max and Freak to the principal's office
11. What Max didn't have until Freak came along
12. The object of the treasure hunt
13. Grim is concerned Max will inherit this from his father.
14. Killer Kane planned to become one to get money.
15. Heroic Biker Babe
16. Freak gives Max a blank one and tells him to fill it with their adventures.

A=	B=	C=	D=
E=	F=	G=	H=
I=	J=	K=	L=
M=	N=	O=	P=

Freak the Mighty Magic Squares 1 Answer Key

Match the definition with the vocabulary word. Put your answers in the magic squares below. When your answers are correct, all columns and rows will add to the same number.

A. SHOULDERS	E. PREACHER	I. PURSE	M. ARTHUR
B. BRAIN	F. GUINEVERE	J. LIFE	N. CHARACTER
C. STRANGLE	G. LORETTA	K. ADDISON	O. GUILTY
D. DONELLI	H. COMICS	L. FLOATING	P. BOOK

1. King ____; once a wimpy little kid, an orphan who pulled a sword from the stone
2. One of the names Kevin uses for his mother
3. Kevin wrapped Max's Christmas present with this.
4. Killer Kane's plea before going to trial
5. How Max feels when he goes to the place in his head
6. Killer Kane's method of killing
7. Freak sits on Max's ___.
8. ____ is dangerous.
9. Principal
10. Sends Max and Freak to the principal's office
11. What Max didn't have until Freak came along
12. The object of the treasure hunt
13. Grim is concerned Max will inherit this from his father.
14. Killer Kane planned to become one to get money.
15. Heroic Biker Babe
16. Freak gives Max a blank one and tells him to fill it with their adventures.

A=7	B=11	C=6	D=10
E=14	F=2	G=15	H=3
I=12	J=8	K=9	L=5
M=1	N=13	O=4	P=16

Freak the Mighty Magic Squares 2

Match the definition with the vocabulary word. Put your answers in the magic squares below. When your answers are correct, all columns and rows will add to the same number.

A. LIFE
B. GUINEVERE
C. FLOUR
D. SEIZURE
E. GRAM
F. COMICS
G. CHARACTER
H. KANE
I. FREAK
J. ICU
K. ADDISON
L. HIM
M. HERO
N. WRITING
O. MILLPOND
P. SHOULDERS

1. Kevin wrapped Max's Christmas present with this.
2. He talks like a dictionary and sits on Max's shoulders.
3. Where Freak the Mighty is born
4. What happens to Freak on his birthday
5. What the police call Max for saving Kevin
6. One of the names Kevin uses for his mother
7. Killer ____; Max's father
8. Principal
9. Max at first only knows King Arthur as the brand of ____ Gram uses.
10. Freak sits on Max's ___.
11. Where Freak dies
12. Max's grandmother
13. Max's father
14. Grim is concerned Max will inherit this from his father.
15. ____ is dangerous.
16. It is like talking, according to Max.

A=	B=	C=	D=
E=	F=	G=	H=
I=	J=	K=	L=
M=	N=	O=	P=

Freak the Mighty Magic Squares 2 Answer Key

Match the definition with the vocabulary word. Put your answers in the magic squares below. When your answers are correct, all columns and rows will add to the same number.

A. LIFE
B. GUINEVERE
C. FLOUR
D. SEIZURE
E. GRAM
F. COMICS
G. CHARACTER
H. KANE
I. FREAK
J. ICU
K. ADDISON
L. HIM
M. HERO
N. WRITING
O. MILLPOND
P. SHOULDERS

1. Kevin wrapped Max's Christmas present with this.
2. He talks like a dictionary and sits on Max's shoulders.
3. Where Freak the Mighty is born
4. What happens to Freak on his birthday
5. What the police call Max for saving Kevin
6. One of the names Kevin uses for his mother
7. Killer ____; Max's father
8. Principal
9. Max at first only knows King Arthur as the brand of ____ Gram uses.
10. Freak sits on Max's ___.
11. Where Freak dies
12. Max's grandmother
13. Max's father
14. Grim is concerned Max will inherit this from his father.
15. ____ is dangerous.
16. It is like talking, according to Max.

A=15	B=6	C=9	D=4
E=12	F=1	G=14	H=7
I=2	J=11	K=8	L=13
M=5	N=16	O=3	P=10

Freak the Mighty Magic Squares 3

Match the definition with the vocabulary word. Put your answers in the magic squares below. When your answers are correct, all columns and rows will add to the same number.

A. SPIVAK
B. GRAM
C. DICTIONARY
D. SHOULDERS
E. MILLPOND
F. ORNITHOPTER
G. MAX
H. GRIM
I. GUILTY
J. PAROLE
K. BOOK
L. GUINEVERE
M. PYRAMID
N. SULFURIC
O. WRITING
P. STRANGLE

1. Freak writes one for Max.
2. Killer Kane violated his ___.
3. Plastic bird
4. It is like talking, according to Max.
5. Killer Kane's method of killing
6. Where Freak the Mighty is born
7. Killer Kane's plea before going to trial
8. Freak sits on Max's ___.
9. Max's Christmas present from Freak is in a box shaped like a ____.
10. He built the Down Under.
11. One of the names Kevin uses for his mother
12. Kevin's doctor
13. Max's grandmother
14. Freak gives Max a blank one and tells him to fill it with their adventures.
15. The Mighty part of Freak the Mighty
16. Freak sprays Killer Kane in the eyes with fake ____ acid.

A=	B=	C=	D=
E=	F=	G=	H=
I=	J=	K=	L=
M=	N=	O=	P=

Freak the Mighty Magic Squares 3 Answer Key

Match the definition with the vocabulary word. Put your answers in the magic squares below. When your answers are correct, all columns and rows will add to the same number.

A. SPIVAK
B. GRAM
C. DICTIONARY
D. SHOULDERS
E. MILLPOND
F. ORNITHOPTER
G. MAX
H. GRIM
I. GUILTY
J. PAROLE
K. BOOK
L. GUINEVERE
M. PYRAMID
N. SULFURIC
O. WRITING
P. STRANGLE

1. Freak writes one for Max.
2. Killer Kane violated his ___.
3. Plastic bird
4. It is like talking, according to Max.
5. Killer Kane's method of killing
6. Where Freak the Mighty is born
7. Killer Kane's plea before going to trial
8. Freak sits on Max's ___.
9. Max's Christmas present from Freak is in a box shaped like a ____.
10. He built the Down Under.
11. One of the names Kevin uses for his mother
12. Kevin's doctor
13. Max's grandmother
14. Freak gives Max a blank one and tells him to fill it with their adventures.
15. The Mighty part of Freak the Mighty
16. Freak sprays Killer Kane in the eyes with fake ____ acid.

A=12	B=13	C=1	D=8
E=6	F=3	G=15	H=10
I=7	J=2	K=14	L=11
M=9	N=16	O=4	P=5

Freak the Mighty Magic Squares 4

Match the definition with the vocabulary word. Put your answers in the magic squares below. When your answers are correct, all columns and rows will add to the same number.

A. SEIZURE
B. HIM
C. KNIGHTS
D. TESTAMENTS
E. SULFURIC
F. GUINEVERE
G. PURSE
H. GRIM
I. GUILTY
J. KANE
K. FREAK
L. WHISTLES
M. BLADE
N. ICU
O. BOOK
P. CHARACTER

1. Where Freak dies
2. The object of the treasure hunt
3. How Freak gets the cops' attention
4. What happens to Freak on his birthday
5. He talks like a dictionary and sits on Max's shoulders.
6. Max's father
7. Tony D's nickname
8. He built the Down Under.
9. Freak sprays Killer Kane in the eyes with fake ____ acid.
10. Grim is concerned Max will inherit this from his father.
11. First human version of robots, according to Freak
12. Killer ____; Max's father
13. Loretta and Iggy live in the New ____.
14. Killer Kane's plea before going to trial
15. One of the names Kevin uses for his mother
16. Freak gives Max a blank one and tells him to fill it with their adventures.

A=	B=	C=	D=
E=	F=	G=	H=
I=	J=	K=	L=
M=	N=	O=	P=

Freak the Mighty Magic Squares 4 Answer Key

Match the definition with the vocabulary word. Put your answers in the magic squares below. When your answers are correct, all columns and rows will add to the same number.

A. SEIZURE
B. HIM
C. KNIGHTS
D. TESTAMENTS
E. SULFURIC
F. GUINEVERE
G. PURSE
H. GRIM
I. GUILTY
J. KANE
K. FREAK
L. WHISTLES
M. BLADE
N. ICU
O. BOOK
P. CHARACTER

1. Where Freak dies
2. The object of the treasure hunt
3. How Freak gets the cops' attention
4. What happens to Freak on his birthday
5. He talks like a dictionary and sits on Max's shoulders.
6. Max's father
7. Tony D's nickname
8. He built the Down Under.
9. Freak sprays Killer Kane in the eyes with fake ____ acid.
10. Grim is concerned Max will inherit this from his father.
11. First human version of robots, according to Freak
12. Killer ____; Max's father
13. Loretta and Iggy live in the New ____.
14. Killer Kane's plea before going to trial
15. One of the names Kevin uses for his mother
16. Freak gives Max a blank one and tells him to fill it with their adventures.

A=4	B=6	C=11	D=13
E=9	F=15	G=2	H=8
I=14	J=12	K=5	L=3
M=7	N=1	O=16	P=10

Freak the Mighty Word Search 1

```
C E L O R A P H I L B R I C K E I A S
O F S R Q C P N B T K J D C I X G D U
M Q T N T N F T R I S M D H C C G D L
I W R I T I N G B O O K G A U A Y I F
C S A T Z H Q R R C A N U R F L F S U
S E N T W Z A E S V W C I A R I Q O R
T I G H O D I H L I V T Q N C E B D N I
N Z L P N Y R P P Z X F E T A U I G C
E U E T X S S M P U Q P V E K R M G P
M R H E X Z H F G R G E R S Q A W X
A E G R N T X C R C L S R R W A R E W
T H I G N I R E B M E M E R G R Y N Y
S D L K Q E C S F X G D W Y B T P V X
E K L G T B W L G Q L H R G L H K G C
T D E I R L O S P U J A R I J U N M M
K A N E P A I N O X N E U D G R I M P
P V O Y T D M H A O H G A Q U L G V W
B Z D I G E S M I C B E P O L X H X J
J N N N P M B T A E R K L P G W T L T
L G X Q I R C E F K R F O E D I S N I
C F F H Z I R I L B K N L O R E T T A
S D P C D P L L X K D W H I S T L E S
```

ADDISON   DONELLI   HERO   MILLPOND   SEIZURE

ARTHUR   EXCALIBUR HIM   ORNITHOPTER SHOULDERS

BIONIC   FLOATING   ICU   PAIN   SPIVAK

BLADE   FLOUR   IGGY   PAROLE   STRANGLE

BOOK   FREAK   INSIDE   PHILBRICK   SULFURIC

BRAIN   GRAM   KANE   PREACHER   TESTAMENTS

CHARACTER GRIM   KNIGHTS PURSE   WHISTLES

COMICS   GUILTY   LIFE   PYRAMID   WRITING

CRETIN   GUINEVERE LORETTA READ

DICTIONARY GWEN   MAX   REMEMBERING

Freak the Mighty Word Search 1 Answer Key

ADDISON	DONELLI	HERO	MILLPOND	SEIZURE
ARTHUR	EXCALIBUR	HIM	ORNITHOPTER	SHOULDERS
BIONIC	FLOATING	ICU	PAIN	SPIVAK
BLADE	FLOUR	IGGY	PAROLE	STRANGLE
BOOK	FREAK	INSIDE	PHILBRICK	SULFURIC
BRAIN	GRAM	KANE	PREACHER	TESTAMENTS
CHARACTER	GRIM	KNIGHTS	PURSE	WHISTLES
COMICS	GUILTY	LIFE	PYRAMID	WRITING
CRETIN	GUINEVERE	LORETTA	READ	
DICTIONARY	GWEN	MAX	REMEMBERING	

Freak the Mighty Word Search 2

```
S P I V A K B T E S T A M E N T S J P
M E G X W N N I P B Q D W R I T I N G
D X U Y P H W I O T O M Y L F M H G G
R C I C Y D I M G N R J I Y H N U Z S
E A N I R D C S E H I Y I L C I N Y P
H L E R A Y P L T Y T C G K L S V F W
C I V U M L L A O L V S G T P P L C M
A B E F I I M A R G E G Y N B O O K G
E U R L D I S U N O M S I H N R R N D
R R E U N H O C I L L A Q J E K E S D
P U R S E L S G T L P E F H M Y T G W
L V I M F C T L H R H F H F A N T T N
S D C J I E R X O E I B S R X C A Z K
E H Z M D R A V P A L X Z E H L V F N
F L O A T I N G T D B Q D A I C U N D
M C L U Q T G Z E R R V R K R Z N R G
G B V N L H L B R R I A W W Y T U L K
L L P L P D E L Z C C K V T L V H R Q
G W E N I T E R C T K B A H I M L U E
N R H S J J W R E X F G P N B W I Q R
F J I Q F Z Y R S N R X J Z E S F R Z
M B B M B R A I N O S I D D A T E F W
```

ADDISON EXCALIBUR HIM ORNITHOPTER SPIVAK

ARTHUR FLOATING ICU PAIN STRANGLE

BIONIC FLOUR IGGY PAROLE SULFURIC

BLADE FREAK INSIDE PHILBRICK TESTAMENTS

BOOK GRAM KANE PREACHER WHISTLES

BRAIN GRIM KNIGHTS PURSE WRITING

CHARACTER GUILTY LIFE PYRAMID

COMICS GUINEVERE LORETTA READ

CRETIN GWEN MAX SEIZURE

DONELLI HERO MILLPOND SHOULDERS

Freak the Mighty Word Search 2 Answer Key

ADDISON	EXCALIBUR	HIM	ORNITHOPTER	SPIVAK
ARTHUR	FLOATING	ICU	PAIN	STRANGLE
BIONIC	FLOUR	IGGY	PAROLE	SULFURIC
BLADE	FREAK	INSIDE	PHILBRICK	TESTAMENTS
BOOK	GRAM	KANE	PREACHER	WHISTLES
BRAIN	GRIM	KNIGHTS	PURSE	WRITING
CHARACTER	GUILTY	LIFE	PYRAMID	
COMICS	GUINEVERE	LORETTA	READ	
CRETIN	GWEN	MAX	SEIZURE	
DONELLI	HERO	MILLPOND	SHOULDERS	

Freak the Mighty Word Search 3

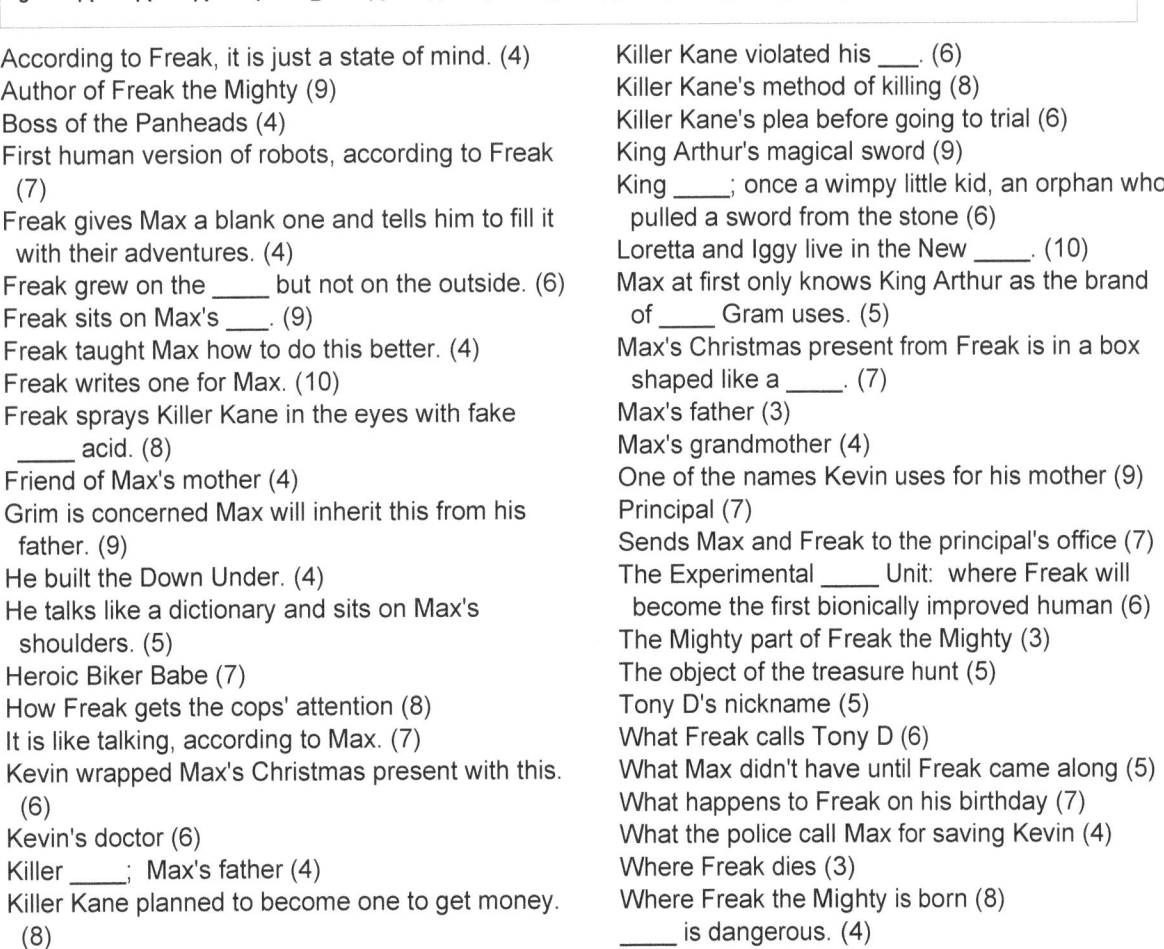

According to Freak, it is just a state of mind. (4)
Author of Freak the Mighty (9)
Boss of the Panheads (4)
First human version of robots, according to Freak (7)
Freak gives Max a blank one and tells him to fill it with their adventures. (4)
Freak grew on the ____ but not on the outside. (6)
Freak sits on Max's ____. (9)
Freak taught Max how to do this better. (4)
Freak writes one for Max. (10)
Freak sprays Killer Kane in the eyes with fake ____ acid. (8)
Friend of Max's mother (4)
Grim is concerned Max will inherit this from his father. (9)
He built the Down Under. (4)
He talks like a dictionary and sits on Max's shoulders. (5)
Heroic Biker Babe (7)
How Freak gets the cops' attention (8)
It is like talking, according to Max. (7)
Kevin wrapped Max's Christmas present with this. (6)
Kevin's doctor (6)
Killer ____; Max's father (4)
Killer Kane planned to become one to get money. (8)

Killer Kane violated his ___. (6)
Killer Kane's method of killing (8)
Killer Kane's plea before going to trial (6)
King Arthur's magical sword (9)
King ____; once a wimpy little kid, an orphan who pulled a sword from the stone (6)
Loretta and Iggy live in the New ____. (10)
Max at first only knows King Arthur as the brand of ____ Gram uses. (5)
Max's Christmas present from Freak is in a box shaped like a ____. (7)
Max's father (3)
Max's grandmother (4)
One of the names Kevin uses for his mother (9)
Principal (7)
Sends Max and Freak to the principal's office (7)
The Experimental ____ Unit: where Freak will become the first bionically improved human (6)
The Mighty part of Freak the Mighty (3)
The object of the treasure hunt (5)
Tony D's nickname (5)
What Freak calls Tony D (6)
What Max didn't have until Freak came along (5)
What happens to Freak on his birthday (7)
What the police call Max for saving Kevin (4)
Where Freak dies (3)
Where Freak the Mighty is born (8)
____ is dangerous. (4)

Freak the Mighty Word Search 3 Answer Key

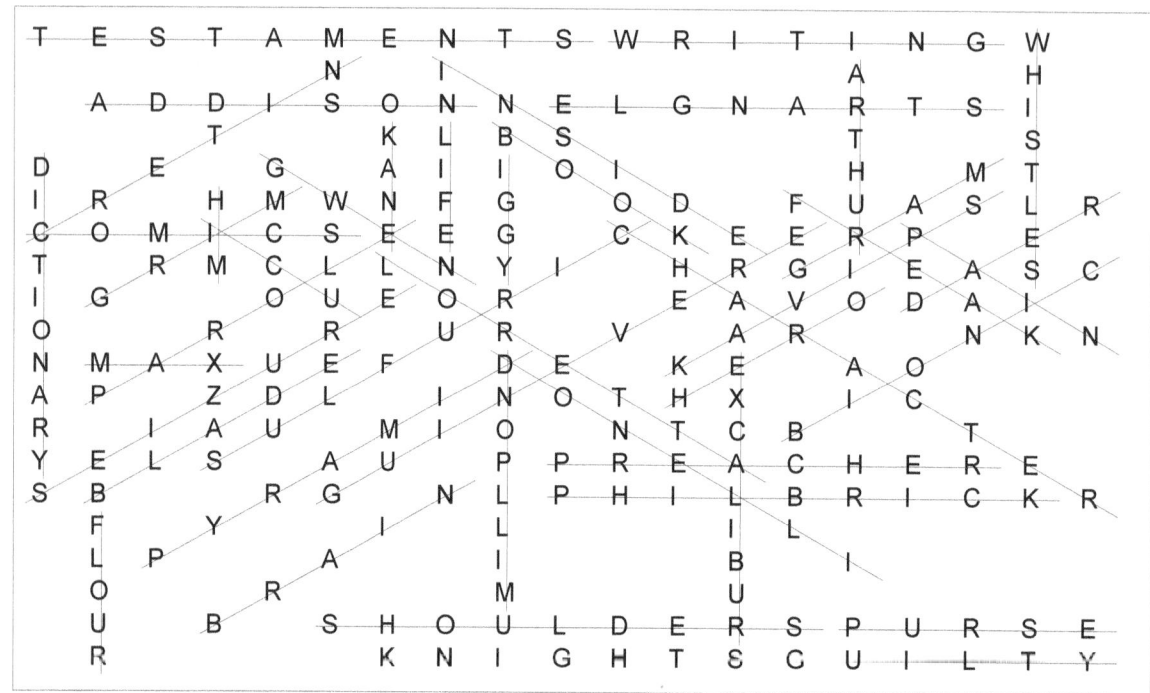

According to Freak, it is just a state of mind. (4)
Author of Freak the Mighty (9)
Boss of the Panheads (4)
First human version of robots, according to Freak (7)
Freak gives Max a blank one and tells him to fill it with their adventures. (4)
Freak grew on the ____ but not on the outside. (6)
Freak sits on Max's ____. (9)
Freak taught Max how to do this better. (4)
Freak writes one for Max. (10)
Freak sprays Killer Kane in the eyes with fake ____ acid. (8)
Friend of Max's mother (4)
Grim is concerned Max will inherit this from his father. (9)
He built the Down Under. (4)
He talks like a dictionary and sits on Max's shoulders. (5)
Heroic Biker Babe (7)
How Freak gets the cops' attention (8)
It is like talking, according to Max. (7)
Kevin wrapped Max's Christmas present with this. (6)
Kevin's doctor (6)
Killer ____; Max's father (4)
Killer Kane planned to become one to get money. (8)

Killer Kane violated his ____. (6)
Killer Kane's method of killing (8)
Killer Kane's plea before going to trial (6)
King Arthur's magical sword (9)
King ____; once a wimpy little kid, an orphan who pulled a sword from the stone (6)
Loretta and Iggy live in the New ____. (10)
Max at first only knows King Arthur as the brand of ____ Gram uses. (5)
Max's Christmas present from Freak is in a box shaped like a ____. (7)
Max's father (3)
Max's grandmother (4)
One of the names Kevin uses for his mother (9)
Principal (7)
Sends Max and Freak to the principal's office (7)
The Experimental ____ Unit: where Freak will become the first bionically improved human (6)
The Mighty part of Freak the Mighty (3)
The object of the treasure hunt (5)
Tony D's nickname (5)
What Freak calls Tony D (6)
What Max didn't have until Freak came along (5)
What happens to Freak on his birthday (7)
What the police call Max for saving Kevin (4)
Where Freak dies (3)
Where Freak the Mighty is born (8)
____ is dangerous. (4)

Freak the Mighty Word Search 4

```
B R A I N W K G L I C U K G W E N S V
B E T X I Z N R I F G A N U P R R P F
K T T V T C I A F N E I R I R U L I J
G C E W E S G M E R R U S N E Z J V J
N A R X R Q H T F E H R W E A I F A Y
D R O S C M T R B T E Z K V C E W K M
W A L G J Y S M R D H N S E H S H G V
C H B T T L E A L L R W J R E I I V B
M C M L F M R U D F Y P K E R N S I Z
I J I V E R O H J D Q U O C P S T G P
R U J R R H F I Q C I R O V F I L G S
G D T E S T A M E N T S B L A D E Y B
K D A N U H G Y X M C E O I O E S H L
F D C A L E Q J X I N A F N O W W X Q
T Z M K F R X Q M S T E E W P N R C H
F Y B C U O M O M I L L P O N D I B C
K L G C R G C A N L L O P Q I R T C M
L Z O W I V X G W I S R P J A S I Z P
M Y D U C L V S D I M A R Y P Y N D W
L G S T R A N G L E Q P T C W D G N S
```

According to Freak, it is just a state of mind. (4)
Boss of the Panheads (4)
First human version of robots, according to Freak (7)
Freak gives Max a blank one and tells him to fill it with their adventures. (4)
Freak grew on the ____ but not on the outside. (6)
Freak sits on Max's ____. (9)
Freak taught Max how to do this better. (4)
Freak sprays Killer Kane in the eyes with fake ____ acid. (8)
Friend of Max's mother (4)
Grim is concerned Max will inherit this from his father. (9)
He built the Down Under. (4)
He talks like a dictionary and sits on Max's shoulders. (5)
Heroic Biker Babe (7)
How Freak gets the cops' attention (8)
How Max feels when he goes to the place in his head (8)
It is like talking, according to Max. (7)
Kevin wrapped Max's Christmas present with this. (6)
Kevin's doctor (6)
Killer ____; Max's father (4)
Killer Kane planned to become one to get money. (8)
Killer Kane violated his ___. (6)
Killer Kane's method of killing (8)
Killer Kane's plea before going to trial (6)
King ____; once a wimpy little kid, an orphan who pulled a sword from the stone (6)
Loretta and Iggy live in the New ____. (10)
Max at first only knows King Arthur as the brand of ____ Gram uses. (5)
Max's Christmas present from Freak is in a box shaped like a ____. (7)
Max's father (3)
Max's grandmother (4)
One of the names Kevin uses for his mother (9)
Principal (7)
Sends Max and Freak to the principal's office (7)
The Experimental ____ Unit: where Freak will become the first bionically improved human (6)
The Mighty part of Freak the Mighty (3)
The object of the treasure hunt (5)
Tony D's nickname (5)
What Freak calls Tony D (6)
What Max didn't have until Freak came along (5)
What happens to Freak on his birthday (7)
What the police call Max for saving Kevin (4)
Where Freak dies (3)
Where Freak the Mighty is born (8)
____ is dangerous. (4)
____ is just an invention of the mind. (11)

Freak the Mighty Word Search 4 Answer Key

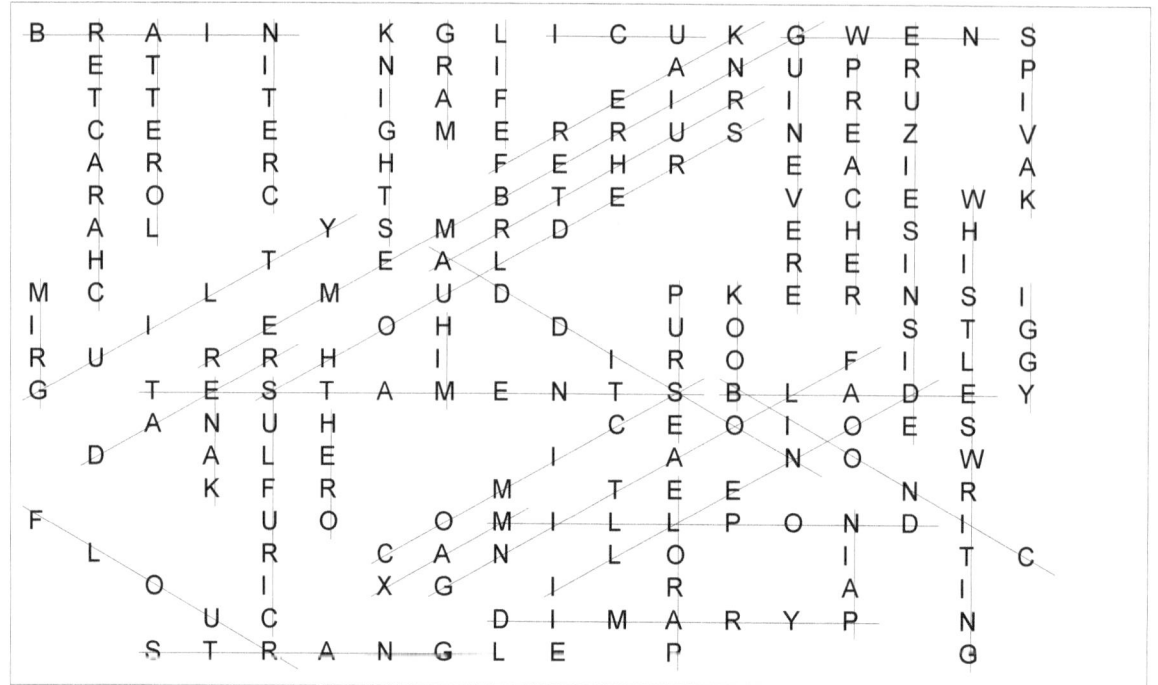

According to Freak, it is just a state of mind. (4)
Boss of the Panheads (4)
First human version of robots, according to Freak (7)
Freak gives Max a blank one and tells him to fill it with their adventures. (4)
Freak grew on the ____ but not on the outside. (6)
Freak sits on Max's ____. (9)
Freak taught Max how to do this better. (4)
Freak sprays Killer Kane in the eyes with fake ____ acid. (8)
Friend of Max's mother (4)
Grim is concerned Max will inherit this from his fathe.r (9)
He built the Down Under. (4)
He talks like a dictionary and sits on Max's shoulders. (5)
Heroic Biker Babe (7)
How Freak gets the cops' attention (8)
How Max feels when he goes to the place in his head (8)
It is like talking, according to Max. (7)
Kevin wrapped Max's Christmas present with this (6)
Kevin's doctor (6)
Killer ____; Max's father (4)
Killer Kane planned to become one to get money. (8)

Killer Kane violated his ____.(6)
Killer Kane's method of killing (8)
Killer Kane's plea before going to trial (6)
King ____; once a wimpy little kid, an orphan who pulled a sword from the stone (6)
Loretta and Iggy live in the New ____. (10)
Max at first only knows King Arthur as the brand of ____ Gram uses. (5)
Max's Christmas present from Freak is in a box shaped like a ____. (7)
Max's father (3)
Max's grandmother (4)
One of the names Kevin uses for his mother (9)
Principal (7)
Sends Max and Freak to the principal's office (7)
The Experimental ____ Unit: where Freak will become the first bionically improved human (6)
The Mighty part of Freak the Mighty (3)
The object of the treasure hunt (5)
Tony D's nickname (5)
What Freak calls Tony D (6)
What Max didn't have until Freak came along (5)
What happens to Freak on his birthday (7)
What the police call Max for saving Kevin (4)
Where Freak dies (3)
Where Freak the Mighty is born (8)
____ is dangerous. (4)
____ is just an invention of the mind. (11)

Freak the Mighty Crossword 1

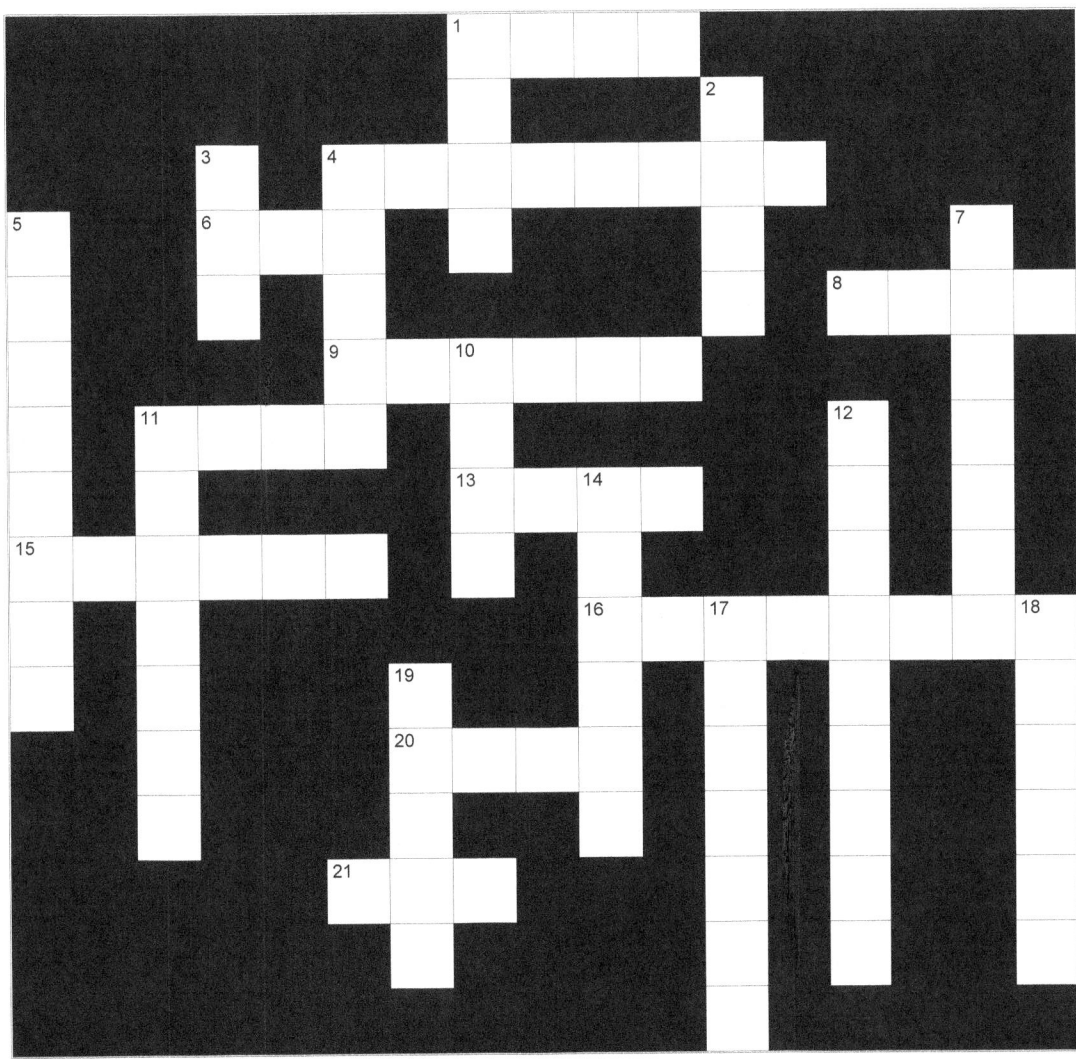

Across
1. Max's grandmother
4. Killer Kane planned to become one to get money.
6. Where Freak dies
8. Freak gives Max a blank one and tells him to fill it with their adventures.
9. Kevin's doctor
11. Killer ____; Max's father
13. He built the Down Under.
15. Killer Kane's plea before going to trial
16. Freak sprays Killer Kane in the eyes with fake ____ acid.
20. Freak taught Max how to do this better.
21. The Mighty part of Freak the Mighty

Down
1. Friend of Max's mother
2. What the police call Max for saving Kevin
3. Max's father
4. The object of the treasure hunt
5. Killer Kane's method of killing
7. Sends Max and Freak to the principal's office
10. Boss of the Panheads
11. First human version of robots, according to Freak
12. Freak sits on Max's ___.
14. Freak grew on the ____ but not on the outside.
17. Heroic Biker Babe
18. Kevin wrapped Max's Christmas present with this.
19. He talks like a dictionary and sits on Max's shoulders.

Freak the Mighty Crossword 1 Answer Key

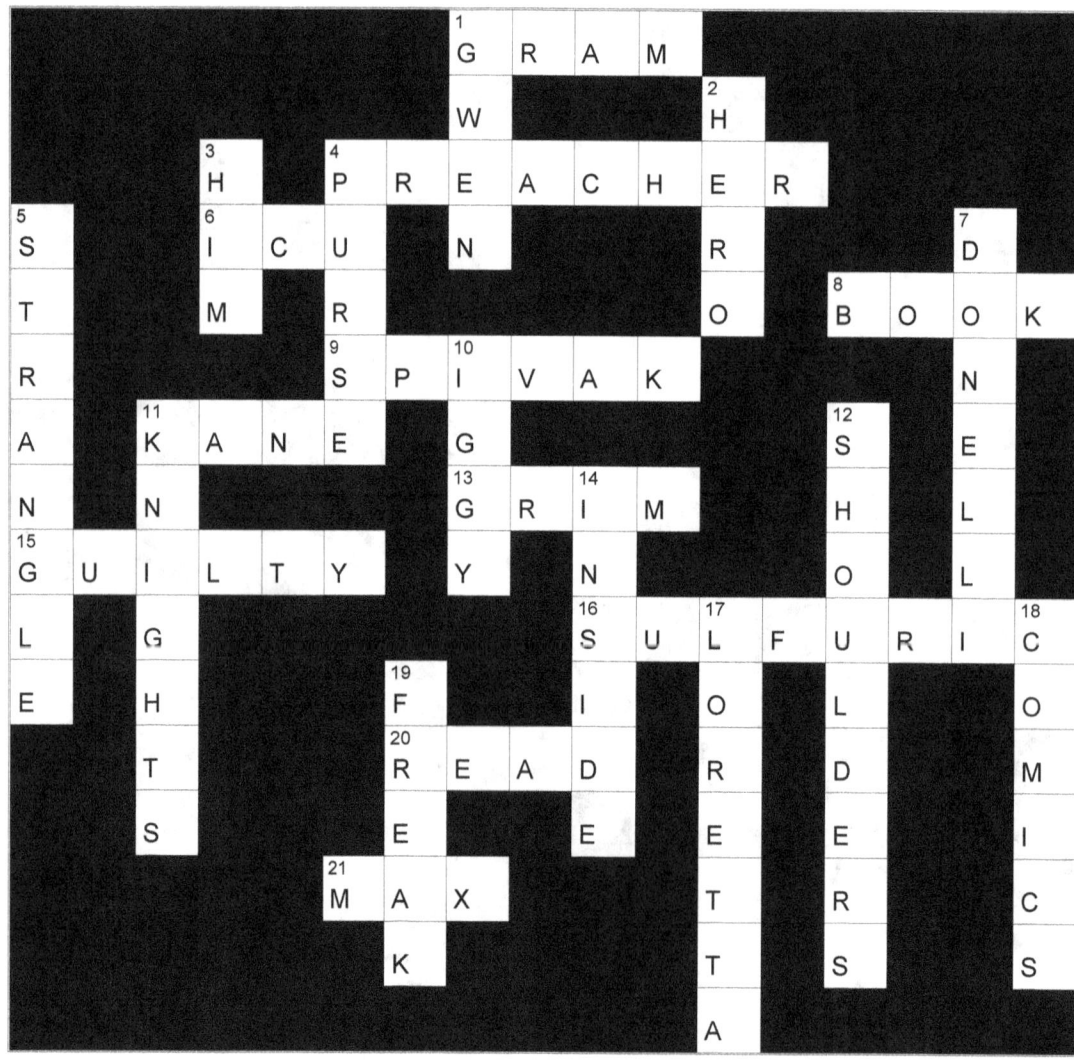

Across
1. Max's grandmother
4. Killer Kane planned to become one to get money.
6. Where Freak dies
8. Freak gives Max a blank one and tells him to fill it with their adventures.
9. Kevin's doctor
11. Killer ____; Max's father
13. He built the Down Under.
15. Killer Kane's plea before going to trial
16. Freak sprays Killer Kane in the eyes with fake ____ acid.
20. Freak taught Max how to do this better.
21. The Mighty part of Freak the Mighty

Down
1. Friend of Max's mother
2. What the police call Max for saving Kevin
3. Max's father
4. The object of the treasure hunt
5. Killer Kane's method of killing
7. Sends Max and Freak to the principal's office
10. Boss of the Panheads
11. First human version of robots, according to Freak
12. Freak sits on Max's ___.
14. Freak grew on the ____ but not on the outside.
17. Heroic Biker Babe
18. Kevin wrapped Max's Christmas present with this.
19. He talks like a dictionary and sits on Max's shoulders.

Freak the Mighty Crossword 2

Across
1. Max's Christmas present from Freak is in a box shaped like a ____.
2. Boss of the Panheads
5. Freak taught Max how to do this better.
7. Where Freak dies
8. Freak sits on Max's ___.
11. Freak gives Max a blank one and tells him to fill it with their adventures.
13. He talks like a dictionary and sits on Max's shoulders.
14. Sends Max and Freak to the principal's office
16. Freak grew on the ____ but not on the outside.
17. Kevin wrapped Max's Christmas present with this.
21. Plastic bird
23. He built the Down Under.
24. Killer Kane's plea before going to trial

Down
1. Author of Freak the Mighty
3. Friend of Max's mother
4. One of the names Kevin uses for his mother
6. King Arthur's magical sword
9. What the police call Max for saving Kevin
10. Killer Kane's method of killing
12. Max at first only knows King Arthur as the brand of ____ Gram uses.
14. Freak writes one for Max.
15. Loretta and Iggy live in the New ____.
18. Where Freak the Mighty is born
19. What Max didn't have until Freak came along
20. Max's father
22. According to Freak, it is just a state of mind.

Freak the Mighty Crossword 2 Answer Key

Across
1. Max's Christmas present from Freak is in a box shaped like a ____.
2. Boss of the Panheads
5. Freak taught Max how to do this better.
7. Where Freak dies
8. Freak sits on Max's ___.
11. Freak gives Max a blank one and tells him to fill it with their adventures.
13. He talks like a dictionary and sits on Max's shoulders.
14. Sends Max and Freak to the principal's office
16. Freak grew on the ____ but not on the outside.
17. Kevin wrapped Max's Christmas present with this.
21. Plastic bird
23. He built the Down Under.
24. Killer Kane's plea before going to trial

Down
1. Author of Freak the Mighty
3. Friend of Max's mother
4. One of the names Kevin uses for his mother
6. King Arthur's magical sword
9. What the police call Max for saving Kevin
10. Killer Kane's method of killing
12. Max at first only knows King Arthur as the brand of ____ Gram uses.
14. Freak writes one for Max.
15. Loretta and Iggy live in the New ____.
18. Where Freak the Mighty is born
19. What Max didn't have until Freak came along
20. Max's father
22. According to Freak, it is just a state of mind.

Freak the Mighty Crossword 3

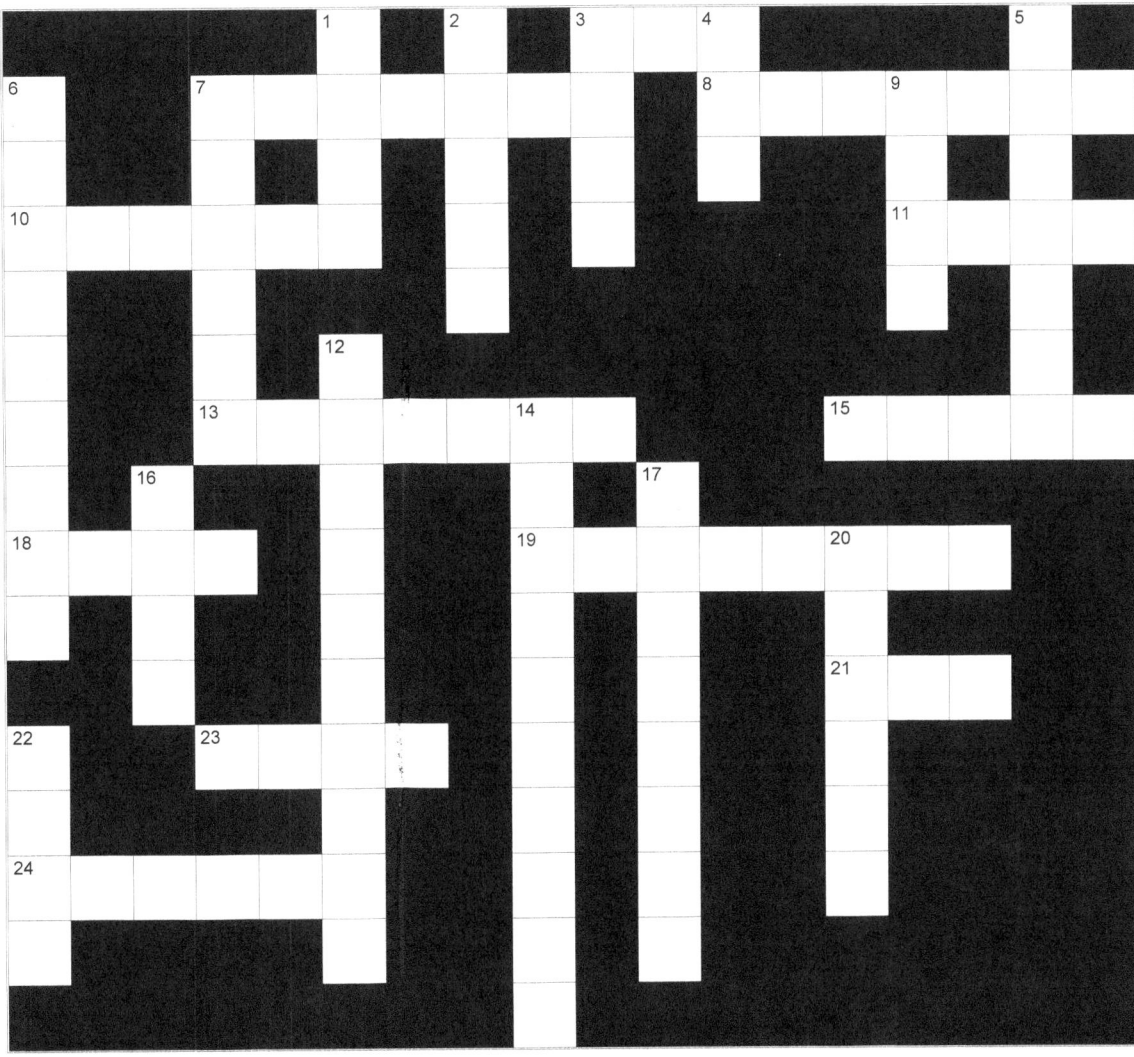

Across
3. Max's father
7. What happens to Freak on his birthday
8. Principal
10. Freak grew on the ____ but not on the outside.
11. Friend of Max's mother
13. First human version of robots, according to Freak
15. What Max didn't have until Freak came along
18. Freak taught Max how to do this better.
19. Killer Kane's method of killing
21. Where Freak dies
23. Killer ____; Max's father
24. King ____; once a wimpy little kid, an orphan who pulled a sword from the stone

Down
1. ____ is dangerous.
2. The object of the treasure hunt
3. What the police call Max for saving Kevin
4. The Mighty part of Freak the Mighty
5. Sends Max and Freak to the principal's office
6. One of the names Kevin uses for his mother
7. Kevin's doctor
9. Boss of the Panheads
12. Freak writes one for Max.
14. Loretta and Iggy live in the New ____.
16. According to Freak, it is just a state of mind.
17. Killer Kane planned to become one to get money.
20. Killer Kane's plea before going to trial
22. Max's grandmother

Freak the Mighty Crossword 3 Answer Key

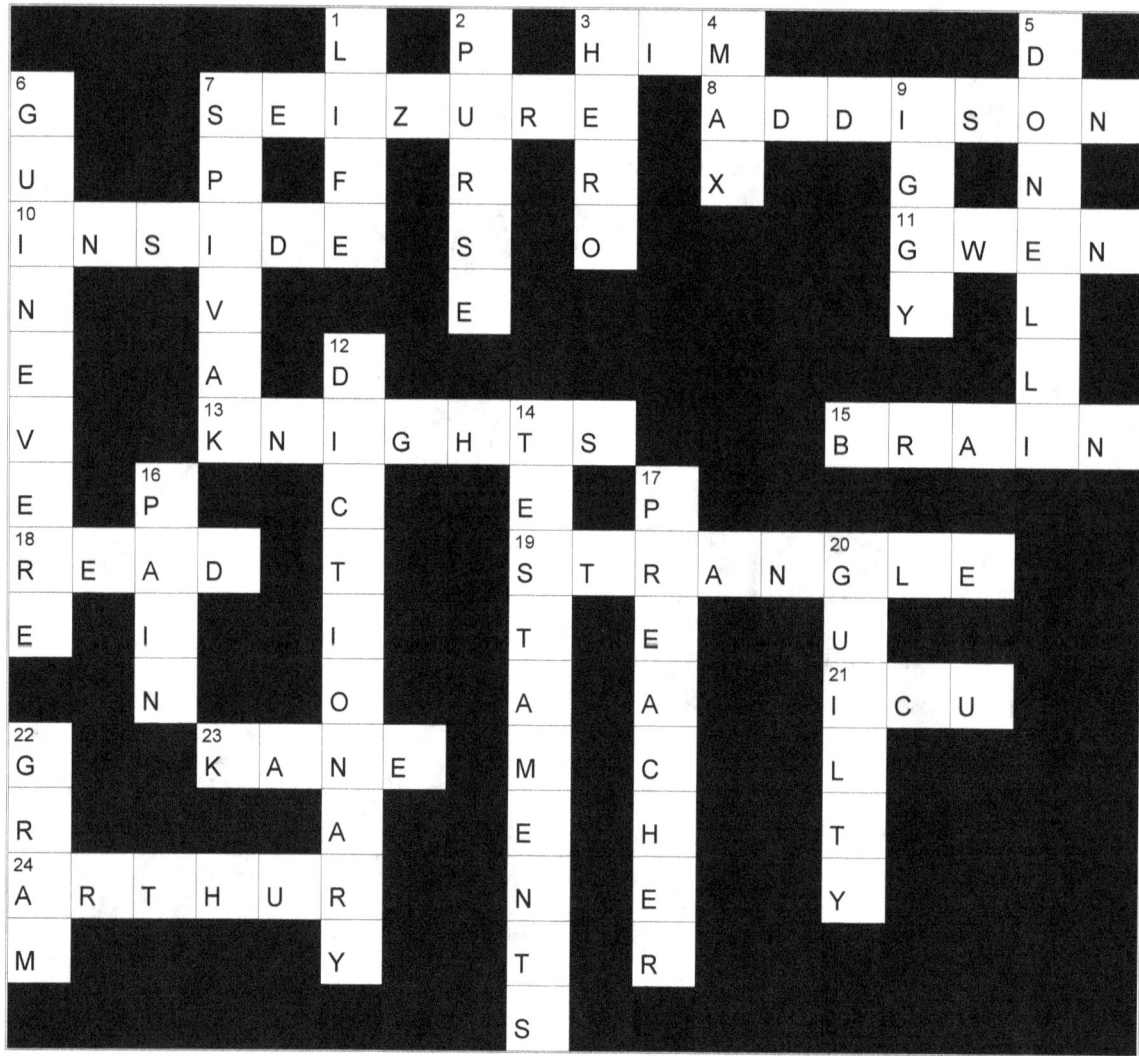

Across
3. Max's father
7. What happens to Freak on his birthday
8. Principal
10. Freak grew on the ____ but not on the outside.
11. Friend of Max's mother
13. First human version of robots, according to Freak
15. What Max didn't have until Freak came along
18. Freak taught Max how to do this better.
19. Killer Kane's method of killing
21. Where Freak dies
23. Killer ____; Max's father
24. King ____; once a wimpy little kid, an orphan who pulled a sword from the stone

Down
1. ____ is dangerous.
2. The object of the treasure hunt
3. What the police call Max for saving Kevin
4. The Mighty part of Freak the Mighty
5. Sends Max and Freak to the principal's office
6. One of the names Kevin uses for his mother
7. Kevin's doctor
9. Boss of the Panheads
12. Freak writes one for Max.
14. Loretta and Iggy live in the New ____.
16. According to Freak, it is just a state of mind.
17. Killer Kane planned to become one to get money.
20. Killer Kane's plea before going to trial
22. Max's grandmother

Freak the Mighty Crossword 4

Across
1. The Experimental ____ Unit: where Freak will become the first bionically improved human
5. Killer ____; Max's father
7. Killer Kane's plea before going to trial
9. According to Freak, it is just a state of mind.
10. The Mighty part of Freak the Mighty
12. Where Freak dies
13. Freak sits on Max's ___.
17. Heroic Biker Babe
19. Freak taught Max how to do this better.
20. The object of the treasure hunt
21. What Max didn't have until Freak came along
22. Max at first only knows King Arthur as the brand of ____ Gram uses.

Down
1. Tony D's nickname
2. Boss of the Panheads
3. Where Freak the Mighty is born
4. Killer Kane's method of killing
6. King Arthur's magical sword
8. Max's father
9. Killer Kane violated his ___.
11. What the police call Max for saving Kevin
13. What happens to Freak on his birthday
14. ____ is dangerous.
15. Freak sprays Killer Kane in the eyes with fake ____ acid.
16. Principal
18. King ____; once a wimpy little kid, an orphan who pulled a sword from the stone

Freak the Mighty Crossword 4 Answer Key

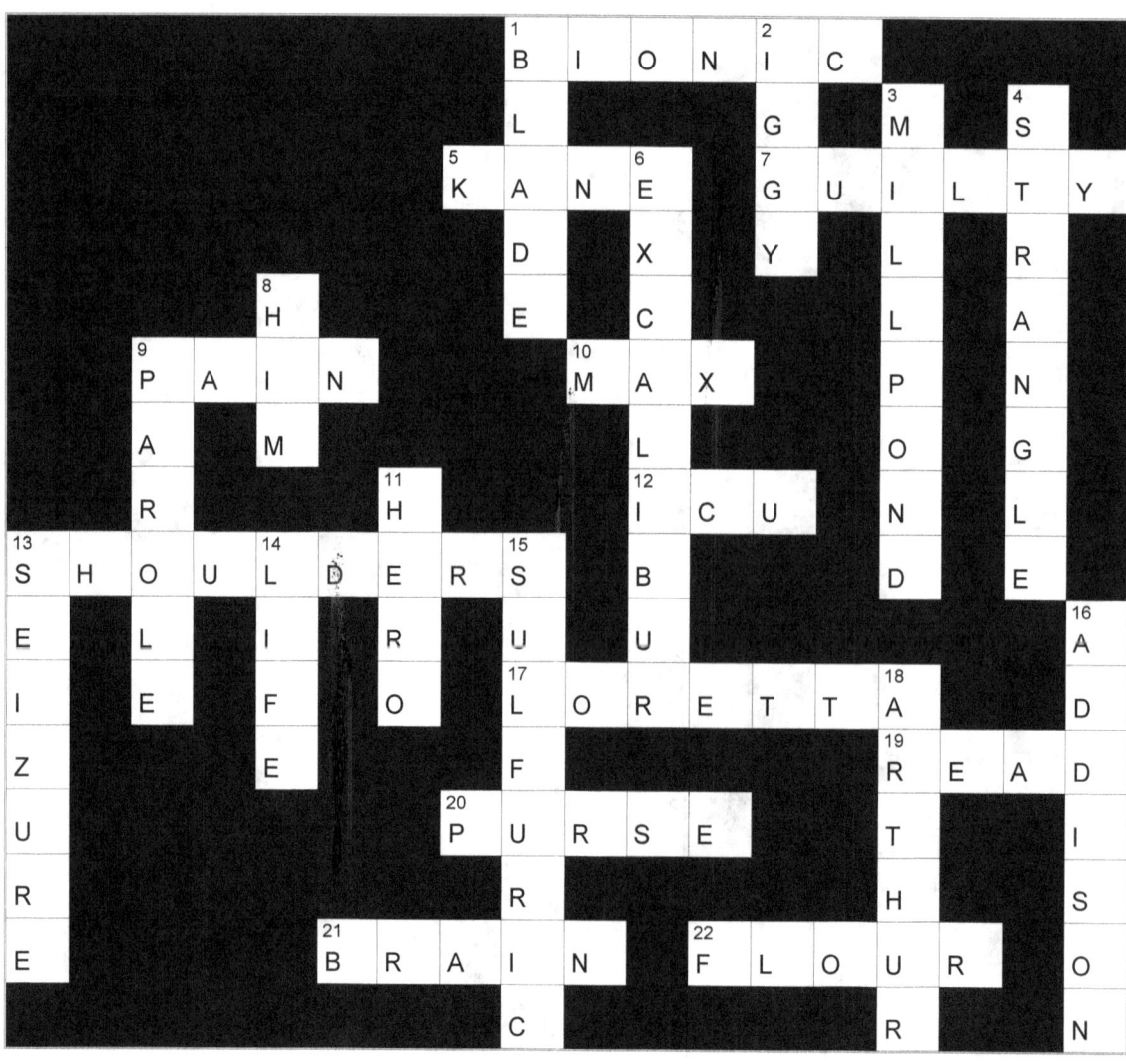

Across
1. The Experimental ____ Unit: where Freak will become the first bionically improved human
5. Kill ____; Max's father
7. Killer Kane's plea before going to trial
9. According to Freak, it is just a state of mind.
10. The Mighty part of Freak the Mighty
12. Where Freak dies
13. Freak sits on Max's ___.
17. Heroic Biker Babe
19. Freak taught Max how to do this better.
20. The object of the treasure hunt
21. What Max didn't have until Freak came along
22. Max at first only knows King Arthur as the brand of ____ Gram uses.

Down
1. Tony D's nickname
2. Boss of the Panheads
3. Where Freak the Mighty is born
4. Killer Kane's method of killing
6. King Arthur's magical sword
8. Max's father
9. Killer Kane violated his ___.
11. What the police call Max for saving Kevin
13. What happens to Freak on his birthday
14. ____ is dangerous.
15. Freak sprays Killer Kane in the eyes with fake ____ acid.
16. Principal
18. King ____; once a wimpy little kid, an orphan who pulled a sword from the stone

Freak the Mighty

WRITING	SEIZURE	ORNITHOPTER	STRANGLE	DONELLI
KANE	BOOK	LORETTA	SHOULDERS	GWEN
BLADE	ARTHUR	FREE SPACE	BIONIC	EXCALIBUR
TESTAMENTS	IGGY	PHILBRICK	DICTIONARY	SPIVAK
GRIM	ICU	GRAM	LIFE	PURSE

Freak the Mighty

MILLPOND	GUILTY	SULFURIC	CHARACTER	COMICS
ADDISON	PREACHER	HERO	REMEMBERING	FLOUR
PAROLE	CRETIN	FREE SPACE	PYRAMID	BRAIN
GUINEVERE	MAX	WHISTLES	FLOATING	PAIN
INSIDE	FREAK	KNIGHTS	PURSE	LIFE

Freak the Mighty

STRANGLE	LORETTA	TESTAMENTS	ARTHUR	KNIGHTS
CRETIN	GWEN	GUINEVERE	DONELLI	CHARACTER
FLOUR	MILLPOND	FREE SPACE	PAIN	SPIVAK
ADDISON	HIM	GRAM	WRITING	WHISTLES
BLADE	SULFURIC	IGGY	INSIDE	ICU

Freak the Mighty

PYRAMID	MAX	FLOATING	SEIZURE	BRAIN
REMEMBERING	READ	PREACHER	FREAK	PURSE
ORNITHOPTER	COMICS	FREE SPACE	PAROLE	DICTIONARY
EXCALIBUR	BIONIC	KANE	GUILTY	PHILBRICK
HERO	GRIM	LIFE	ICU	INSIDE

Freak the Mighty

KANE	KNIGHTS	FLOUR	WRITING	DONELLI
BRAIN	MILLPOND	GRAM	FREAK	COMICS
BLADE	READ	FREE SPACE	TESTAMENTS	PREACHER
MAX	LIFE	GWEN	GUINEVERE	GUILTY
SEIZURE	LORETTA	ADDISON	IGGY	STRANGLE

Freak the Mighty

HIM	SULFURIC	GRIM	INSIDE	ARTHUR
SPIVAK	HERO	BIONIC	PHILBRICK	SHOULDERS
PYRAMID	CHARACTER	FREE SPACE	DICTIONARY	ORNITHOPTER
BOOK	WHISTLES	PAROLE	PAIN	FLOATING
PURSE	CRETIN	REMEMBERING	STRANGLE	IGGY

Freak the Mighty

CHARACTER	GWEN	PYRAMID	BOOK	KNIGHTS
ICU	HIM	DICTIONARY	BRAIN	COMICS
BLADE	PAROLE	FREE SPACE	BIONIC	FLOATING
GRIM	ORNITHOPTER	PREACHER	PHILBRICK	LORETTA
WRITING	IGGY	REMEMBERING	MAX	PURSE

Freak the Mighty

LIFE	KANE	DONELLI	ARTHUR	WHISTLES
SULFURIC	MILLPOND	PAIN	GUILTY	EXCALIBUR
SEIZURE	STRANGLE	FREE SPACE	SPIVAK	SHOULDERS
GUINEVERE	INSIDE	FLOUR	FREAK	HERO
CRETIN	TESTAMENTS	GRAM	PURSE	MAX

Freak the Mighty

HERO	BOOK	TESTAMENTS	DONELLI	FLOATING
REMEMBERING	SHOULDERS	DICTIONARY	INSIDE	WRITING
LORETTA	GRIM	FREE SPACE	GUINEVERE	ADDISON
PHILBRICK	BLADE	FLOUR	KNIGHTS	LIFE
ARTHUR	MILLPOND	CHARACTER	GWEN	KANE

Freak the Mighty

GRAM	CRETIN	HIM	PYRAMID	SULFURIC
EXCALIBUR	COMICS	STRANGLE	BRAIN	ICU
ORNITHOPTER	FREAK	FREE SPACE	GUILTY	SPIVAK
IGGY	READ	BIONIC	PREACHER	SEIZURE
PAROLE	PAIN	MAX	KANE	GWEN

Freak the Mighty

MAX	BRAIN	ADDISON	PYRAMID	BOOK
PAIN	PURSE	SHOULDERS	ORNITHOPTER	ICU
HIM	GWEN	FREE SPACE	GUILTY	TESTAMENTS
LIFE	DONELLI	GUINEVERE	WHISTLES	FLOUR
CRETIN	DICTIONARY	DIONIC	KNIGHTS	BLADE

Freak the Mighty

ARTHUR	COMICS	SEIZURE	GRIM	PHILBRICK
WRITING	READ	INSIDE	IGGY	CHARACTER
SPIVAK	PREACHER	FREE SPACE	MILLPOND	FLOATING
LORETTA	GRAM	FREAK	PAROLE	REMEMBERING
HERO	STRANGLE	KANE	BLADE	KNIGHTS

Freak the Mighty

PREACHER	KANE	DICTIONARY	WHISTLES	GUILTY
REMEMBERING	PYRAMID	MILLPOND	FREAK	TESTAMENTS
CHARACTER	SEIZURE	FREE SPACE	PHILBRICK	HIM
STRANGLE	GRAM	ARTHUR	SPIVAK	EXCALIBUR
GRIM	KNIGHTS	FLOUR	LORETTA	GWEN

Freak the Mighty

PURSE	BOOK	LIFE	BIONIC	ADDISON
PAROLE	BRAIN	CRETIN	IGGY	FLOATING
WRITING	INSIDE	FREE SPACE	READ	SHOULDERS
PAIN	ICU	COMICS	MAX	SULFURIC
BLADE	GUINEVERE	DONELLI	GWEN	LORETTA

Freak the Mighty

IGGY	PAIN	GRIM	ARTHUR	GRAM
COMICS	KANE	DICTIONARY	REMEMBERING	PHILBRICK
KNIGHTS	PYRAMID	FREE SPACE	INSIDE	LORETTA
HIM	SEIZURE	PAROLE	GUINEVERE	WHISTLES
BRAIN	READ	BLADE	CRETIN	FLOATING

Freak the Mighty

DONELLI	SPIVAK	WRITING	PURSE	ICU
SHOULDERS	BIONIC	GWEN	EXCALIBUR	FLOUR
SULFURIC	LIFE	FREE SPACE	MILLPOND	MAX
STRANGLE	ORNITHOPTER	GUILTY	FREAK	PREACHER
ADDISON	CHARACTER	HERO	FLOATING	CRETIN

Freak the Mighty

BIONIC	STRANGLE	SPIVAK	PAIN	LIFE
CRETIN	GUILTY	ICU	PHILBRICK	PYRAMID
PURSE	FLOATING	FREE SPACE	GRAM	SULFURIC
BRAIN	REMEMBERING	ARTHUR	INSIDE	TESTAMENTS
HIM	WHISTLES	SHOULDERS	CHARACTER	WRITING

Freak the Mighty

GWEN	READ	HERO	GUINEVERE	PREACHER
GRIM	PAROLE	BLADE	FLOUR	COMICS
DICTIONARY	FREAK	FREE SPACE	SEIZURE	MAX
KNIGHTS	LORETTA	EXCALIBUR	IGGY	BOOK
MILLPOND	ADDISON	KANE	WRITING	CHARACTER

Freak the Mighty

COMICS	CRETIN	DICTIONARY	FLOUR	WHISTLES
EXCALIBUR	HIM	BLADE	LORETTA	DONELLI
LIFE	BOOK	FREE SPACE	BIONIC	REMEMBERING
PYRAMID	FREAK	BRAIN	SEIZURE	SULFURIC
PURSE	PHILBRICK	INSIDE	KANE	SPIVAK

Freak the Mighty

KNIGHTS	MILLPOND	GWEN	ARTHUR	HERO
ICU	TESTAMENTS	FLOATING	PAIN	PREACHER
MAX	IGGY	FREE SPACE	GUINEVERE	ADDISON
SHOULDERS	GUILTY	CHARACTER	READ	WRITING
ORNITHOPTER	GRIM	STRANGLE	SPIVAK	KANE

Freak the Mighty

REMEMBERING	ARTHUR	MAX	DICTIONARY	WRITING
FLOATING	INSIDE	TESTAMENTS	PHILBRICK	FREAK
SULFURIC	EXCALIBUR	FREE SPACE	DONELLI	HIM
PURSE	GWEN	IGGY	ADDISON	BRAIN
LIFE	CHARACTER	KNIGHTS	ICU	KANE

Freak the Mighty

PYRAMID	SPIVAK	GUINEVERE	LORETTA	ORNITHOPTER
BOOK	PREACHER	GRIM	PAIN	SEIZURE
PAROLE	WHISTLES	FREE SPACE	HERO	BLADE
COMICS	MILLPOND	BIONIC	CRETIN	GUILTY
FLOUR	READ	STRANGLE	KANE	ICU

Freak the Mighty

WHISTLES	BOOK	REMEMBERING	ADDISON	TESTAMENTS
ICU	LORETTA	PHILBRICK	CHARACTER	HIM
EXCALIBUR	COMICS	FREE SPACE	READ	BLADE
GRAM	CRETIN	GRIM	PREACHER	PAROLE
FLOUR	WRITING	GUINEVERE	SHOULDERS	PURSE

Freak the Mighty

PYRAMID	ORNITHOPTER	MAX	FLOATING	PAIN
GWEN	INSIDE	GUILTY	LIFE	SULFURIC
STRANGLE	DONELLI	FREE SPACE	ARTHUR	IGGY
BIONIC	DICTIONARY	FREAK	HERO	KNIGHTS
KANE	MILLPOND	SEIZURE	PURSE	SHOULDERS

Freak the Mighty

GWEN	BRAIN	ADDISON	IGGY	MILLPOND
FLOUR	GRIM	LORETTA	ICU	CRETIN
COMICS	GRAM	FREE SPACE	GUINEVERE	LIFE
HERO	WRITING	INSIDE	SPIVAK	SHOULDERS
DICTIONARY	SULFURIC	PURSE	TESTAMENTS	BLADE

Freak the Mighty

FREAK	REMEMBERING	PAIN	PREACHER	PAROLE
EXCALIBUR	CHARACTER	KANE	WHISTLES	FLOATING
MAX	PYRAMID	FREE SPACE	SEIZURE	ARTHUR
ORNITHOPTER	STRANGLE	PHILBRICK	GUILTY	DONELLI
BOOK	READ	KNIGHTS	BLADE	TESTAMENTS

Freak the Mighty

LORETTA	PAROLE	GRIM	PHILBRICK	INSIDE
EXCALIBUR	FREAK	PAIN	DONELLI	HIM
STRANGLE	REMEMBERING	FREE SPACE	CRETIN	FLOATING
MAX	IGGY	KANE	SEIZURE	BLADE
GUINEVERE	SPIVAK	SHOULDERS	ICU	MILLPOND

Freak the Mighty

BIONIC	BOOK	READ	ORNITHOPTER	SULFURIC
CHARACTER	BRAIN	PURSE	PYRAMID	LIFE
ADDISON	WHISTLES	FREE SPACE	ARTHUR	WRITING
GRAM	PREACHER	KNIGHTS	COMICS	GUILTY
GWEN	HERO	DICTIONARY	MILLPOND	ICU

Freak the Mighty

ICU	CHARACTER	PAROLE	FREAK	TESTAMENTS
PHILBRICK	MAX	INSIDE	KANE	BIONIC
CRETIN	FLOATING	FREE SPACE	MILLPOND	SULFURIC
REMEMBERING	ADDISON	GRIM	COMICS	SHOULDERS
LIFE	BOOK	BRAIN	SPIVAK	HIM

Freak the Mighty

READ	DONELLI	BLADE	SEIZURE	GWEN
WHISTLES	STRANGLE	HERO	GUINEVERE	KNIGHTS
LORETTA	PREACHER	FREE SPACE	ARTHUR	WRITING
PYRAMID	IGGY	DICTIONARY	EXCALIBUR	FLOUR
ORNITHOPTER	GRAM	GUILTY	HIM	SPIVAK

Freak the Mighty

HIM	PYRAMID	FLOATING	WHISTLES	CHARACTER
MILLPOND	BIONIC	BLADE	SULFURIC	BOOK
FLOUR	SPIVAK	FREE SPACE	LIFE	GRAM
LORETTA	REMEMBERING	PURSE	GUILTY	SEIZURE
DONELLI	ARTHUR	STRANGLE	GUINEVERE	READ

Freak the Mighty

SHOULDERS	FREAK	COMICS	CRETIN	ORNITHOPTER
ADDISON	PAROLE	PHILBRICK	MAX	BRAIN
GWEN	WRITING	FREE SPACE	GRIM	PAIN
DICTIONARY	KANE	HERO	IGGY	PREACHER
EXCALIBUR	KNIGHTS	TESTAMENTS	READ	GUINEVERE

Freak the Mighty Vocabulary Word List

No.	Word	Clue/Definition
1.	ABDUCT	Take (someone) away illegally by force or deception
2.	ABERRATION	Unwelcome deviation from normal
3.	ACCOMMODATIONS	Living space; lodgings
4.	ALTERNATIVES	Choices
5.	ARCHETYPE	An original model
6.	AUTOMATIC	Working by itself with little or no direct human control
7.	CAMOUFLAGE	Protective coloring or disguise
8.	CONSEQUENCES	Results of one's actions
9.	CONVERGING	Coming together in one place
10.	CORROSIVE	Capable of destroying slowly by chemical action
11.	DELIGHTED	Very happy
12.	DEMEANOR	The way a person behaves
13.	DETENTION	Punishment of being kept in school after hours
14.	DIVULGED	Made known; revealed
15.	DYSFUNCTIONAL	Not operating normally or properly
16.	DYSLEXIC	Having difficulty interpreting words, letters, and symbols
17.	EMBARRASSED	To feel self-conscious or ill at ease
18.	ESPECIALLY	To a great degree; very much
19.	EVASIVE	Tending or intended to avoid
20.	EXPEL	Eject forcefully
21.	EXPRESSION	Word or phrase communicating an idea
22.	FACILITATE	Make easier
23.	FEALTY	Loyalty; faithfulness
24.	FIERCE	Violent or aggressive; ferocious
25.	FRANTIC	Conducted in a hurried and chaotic way; full of fear or anxiety
26.	FUNCTIONAL	Useful; practical; working
27.	FURROWED	Trenched; rutted; grooved; wrinkled
28.	HOODLUM	Tough and aggressive young man
29.	HYPNOTIZED	Put into a trance
30.	IGNORANT	Lacking knowledge
31.	INJUSTICE	Something unfair and wrong
32.	INTENSIVE	Concentrated; thorough
33.	INTERVENTION	Action taken to improve a medical disorder
34.	INVENTION	Something newly created
35.	MANIFESTATION	Object that shows or embodies something
36.	MIRACULOUS	Like a miracle; happening without any natural or scientific explanation
37.	MORON	Stupid person
38.	OATH	Solemn promise
39.	OBLIGATION	Duty
40.	OBNOXIOUS	Extremely unpleasant
41.	OPTIMUM	Most favorable; best
42.	PARALYZED	Caused to be incapable of movement
43.	PARTICULAR	Specific; a certain one
44.	PERSPECTIVE	A view or outlook
45.	PHONY	Fake
46.	POSSESSED	Controlled as if by a spirit or other force
47.	PRECAUTION	Measure taken in advance to prevent something undesirable from happening
48.	PRECIOUS	Valuable; having great value
49.	PRODIGY	Young person with exceptional abilities

Freak the Mighty Vocabulary Word List Continued

No.	Word	Clue/Definition
50.	PROPULSION	Force that sends forward
51.	PYRAMID	Structure with a square or triangular base and sloping sides that meet in a point at the top
52.	REGURGITATE	To vomit
53.	REMARKABLE	Uncommon; worthy of notice
54.	RETRIEVAL	Act or process of getting something back
55.	RINGER	Informal term for a person's double
56.	SCUTTLE	Run hurriedly with short, quick steps
57.	SOBRIQUET	Nickname
58.	STABILIZED	Balanced; made less likely to fall
59.	STEED	Horse
60.	TELEMETRY	Transmission of readings to a distant receiving set or station
61.	TEMPORARY	Not lasting
62.	TENEMENTS	Apartment houses over-crowded and poorly maintained
63.	TRACHEOTOMY	Incision in the windpipe made to relieve an obstruction to breathing
64.	TRAJECTORY	The path of a moving body or particle
65.	TROUSERS	Pants
66.	TRUSSED	Tied up
67.	UNIQUE	One of a kind
68.	URGENCY	Need for immediate attention or action
69.	VIOLATE	Break or fail to comply with a rule or agreement

Copyrighted

Freak the Mighty Vocabulary Fill In The Blanks 1

1. Eject forcefully
2. Act or process of getting something back
3. Uncommon; worthy of notice
4. Made known; revealed
5. Stupid person
6. Informal term for a person's double
7. Take (someone) away illegally by force or deception
8. Action taken to improve a medical disorder
9. Violent or aggressive; ferocious
10. Run hurriedly with short, quick steps
11. Controlled as if by a spirit or other force
12. Choices
13. Living space; lodgings
14. Specific; a certain one
15. Horse
16. The way a person behaves
17. Measure taken in advance to prevent something undesirable from happening
18. Extremely unpleasant
19. Valuable; having great value
20. Trenched; rutted; grooved; wrinkled

Freak the Mighty Vocabulary Fill In The Blanks 1 Answer Key

EXPEL	1. Eject forcefully
RETRIEVAL	2. Act or process of getting something back
REMARKABLE	3. Uncommon; worthy of notice
DIVULGED	4. Made known; revealed
MORON	5. Stupid person
RINGER	6. Informal term for a person's double
ABDUCT	7. Take (someone) away illegally by force or deception
INTERVENTION	8. Action taken to improve a medical disorder
FIERCE	9. Violent or aggressive; ferocious
SCUTTLE	10. Run hurriedly with short, quick steps
POSSESSED	11. Controlled as if by a spirit or other force
ALTERNATIVES	12. Choices
ACCOMMODATIONS	13. Living space; lodgings
PARTICULAR	14. Specific; a certain one
STEED	15. Horse
DEMEANOR	16. The way a person behaves
PRECAUTION	17. Measure taken in advance to prevent something undesirable from happening
OBNOXIOUS	18. Extremely unpleasant
PRECIOUS	19. Valuable; having great value
FURROWED	20. Trenched; rutted; grooved; wrinkled

Freak the Mighty Vocabulary Fill In The Blanks 2

1. Something unfair and wrong
2. Young person with exceptional abilities
3. Results of one's actions
4. Loyalty; faithfulness
5. Make easier
6. Informal term for a person's double
7. Pants
8. Specific; a certain one
9. A view or outlook
10. Caused to be incapable of movement
11. Action taken to improve a medical disorder
12. Protective coloring or disguise
13. One of a kind
14. Working by itself with little or no direct human control
15. Apartment houses over-crowded and poorly maintained
16. Like a miracle; happening without any natural or scientific explanation
17. Controlled as if by a spirit or other force
18. Valuable; having great value
19. Incision in the windpipe made to relieve an obstruction to breathing
20. Extremely unpleasant

Freak the Mighty Vocabulary Fill In The Blanks 2 Answer Key

INJUSTICE	1. Something unfair and wrong
PRODIGY	2. Young person with exceptional abilities
CONSEQUENCES	3. Results of one's actions
FEALTY	4. Loyalty; faithfulness
FACILITATE	5. Make easier
RINGER	6. Informal term for a person's double
TROUSERS	7. Pants
PARTICULAR	8. Specific; a certain one
PERSPECTIVE	9. A view or outlook
PARALYZED	10. Caused to be incapable of movement
INTERVENTION	11. Action taken to improve a medical disorder
CAMOUFLAGE	12. Protective coloring or disguise
UNIQUE	13. One of a kind
AUTOMATIC	14. Working by itself with little or no direct human control
TENEMENTS	15. Apartment houses over-crowded and poorly maintained
MIRACULOUS	16. Like a miracle; happening without any natural or scientific explanation
POSSESSED	17. Controlled as if by a spirit or other force
PRECIOUS	18. Valuable; having great value
TRACHEOTOMY	19. Incision in the windpipe made to relieve an obstruction to breathing
OBNOXIOUS	20. Extremely unpleasant

Freak the Mighty Vocabulary Fill In The Blanks 3

1. Most favorable; best
2. Apartment houses over-crowded and poorly maintained
3. Uncommon; worthy of notice
4. To a great degree; very much
5. Conducted in a hurried and chaotic way; full of fear or anxiety
6. Controlled as if by a spirit or other force
7. The way a person behaves
8. A view or outlook
9. Something unfair and wrong
10. Young person with exceptional abilities
11. Force that sends forward
12. Protective coloring or disguise
13. An original model
14. Like a miracle; happening without any natural or scientific explanation
15. Incision in the windpipe made to relieve an obstruction to breathing
16. Make easier
17. One of a kind
18. Need for immediate attention or action
19. Specific; a certain one
20. Results of one's actions

Freak the Mighty Vocabulary Fill In The Blanks 3 Answer Key

OPTIMUM	1. Most favorable; best
TENEMENTS	2. Apartment houses over-crowded and poorly maintained
REMARKABLE	3. Uncommon; worthy of notice
ESPECIALLY	4. To a great degree; very much
FRANTIC	5. Conducted in a hurried and chaotic way; full of fear or anxiety
POSSESSED	6. Controlled as if by a spirit or other force
DEMEANOR	7. The way a person behaves
PERSPECTIVE	8. A view or outlook
INJUSTICE	9. Something unfair and wrong
PRODIGY	10. Young person with exceptional abilities
PROPULSION	11. Force that sends forward
CAMOUFLAGE	12. Protective coloring or disguise
ARCHETYPE	13. An original model
MIRACULOUS	14. Like a miracle; happening without any natural or scientific explanation
TRACHEOTOMY	15. Incision in the windpipe made to relieve an obstruction to breathing
FACILITATE	16. Make easier
UNIQUE	17. One of a kind
URGENCY	18. Need for immediate attention or action
PARTICULAR	19. Specific; a certain one
CONSEQUENCES	20. Results of one's actions

Freak the Mighty Vocabulary Fill In The Blanks 4

_____ 1. Specific; a certain one

_____ 2. Controlled as if by a spirit or other force

_____ 3. Unwelcome deviation from normal

_____ 4. An original model

_____ 5. The path of a moving body or particle

_____ 6. Structure with a square or triangular base and sloping sides that meet in a point at the top

_____ 7. Violent or aggressive; ferocious

_____ 8. Caused to be incapable of movement

_____ 9. Run hurriedly with short, quick steps

_____ 10. Very happy

_____ 11. Make easier

_____ 12. Need for immediate attention or action

_____ 13. Pants

_____ 14. Living space; lodgings

_____ 15. Valuable; having great value

_____ 16. Break or fail to comply with a rule or agreement

_____ 17. Put into a trance

_____ 18. Act or process of getting something back

_____ 19. Solemn promise

_____ 20. Incision in the windpipe made to relieve an obstruction to breathing

Freak the Mighty Vocabulary Fill In The Blanks 4 Answer Key

PARTICULAR	1. Specific; a certain one
POSSESSED	2. Controlled as if by a spirit or other force
ABERRATION	3. Unwelcome deviation from normal
ARCHETYPE	4. An original model
TRAJECTORY	5. The path of a moving body or particle
PYRAMID	6. Structure with a square or triangular base and sloping sides that meet in a point at the top
FIERCE	7. Violent or aggressive; ferocious
PARALYZED	8. Caused to be incapable of movement
SCUTTLE	9. Run hurriedly with short, quick steps
DELIGHTED	10. Very happy
FACILITATE	11. Make easier
URGENCY	12. Need for immediate attention or action
TROUSERS	13. Pants
ACCOMMODATIONS	14. Living space; lodgings
PRECIOUS	15. Valuable; having great value
VIOLATE	16. Break or fail to comply with a rule or agreement
HYPNOTIZED	17. Put into a trance
RETRIEVAL	18. Act or process of getting something back
OATH	19. Solemn promise
TRACHEOTOMY	20. Incision in the windpipe made to relieve an obstruction to breathing

Freak the Mighty Vocabulary Matching 1

___ 1. DYSLEXIC   A. Apartment houses over-crowded and poorly maintained
___ 2. EXPRESSION   B. Act or process of getting something back
___ 3. FIERCE   C. Very happy
___ 4. MANIFESTATION   D. Useful; practical; working
___ 5. DETENTION   E. Word or phrase communicating an idea
___ 6. CONSEQUENCES   F. Extremely unpleasant
___ 7. FUNCTIONAL   G. Eject forcefully
___ 8. ARCHETYPE   H. Having difficulty interpreting words, letters, and symbols
___ 9. INTENSIVE   I. Loyalty; faithfulness
___10. TENEMENTS   J. Conducted in a hurried and chaotic way; full of fear or anxiety
___11. RETRIEVAL   K. Results of one's actions
___12. FEALTY   L. Need for immediate attention or action
___13. PARTICULAR   M. Object that shows or embodies something
___14. EXPEL   N. Specific; a certain one
___15. EMBARRASSED   O. Caused to be incapable of movement
___16. PRECIOUS   P. Concentrated; thorough
___17. DELIGHTED   Q. To feel self-conscious or ill at ease
___18. PARALYZED   R. Violent or aggressive; ferocious
___19. HOODLUM   S. Tough and aggressive young man
___20. URGENCY   T. Punishment of being kept in school after hours
___21. CORROSIVE   U. Capable of destroying slowly by chemical action
___22. ABERRATION   V. Valuable; having great value
___23. POSSESSED   W. Controlled as if by a spirit or other force
___24. OBNOXIOUS   X. Unwelcome deviation from normal
___25. FRANTIC   Y. An original model

Freak the Mighty Vocabulary Matching 1 Answer Key

H - 1.	DYSLEXIC	A. Apartment houses over-crowded and poorly maintained
E - 2.	EXPRESSION	B. Act or process of getting something back
R - 3.	FIERCE	C. Very happy
M - 4.	MANIFESTATION	D. Useful; practical; working
T - 5.	DETENTION	E. Word or phrase communicating an idea
K - 6.	CONSEQUENCES	F. Extremely unpleasant
D - 7.	FUNCTIONAL	G. Eject forcefully
Y - 8.	ARCHETYPE	H. Having difficulty interpreting words, letters, and symbols
P - 9.	INTENSIVE	I. Loyalty; faithfulness
A - 10.	TENEMENTS	J. Conducted in a hurried and chaotic way; full of fear or anxiety
B - 11.	RETRIEVAL	K. Results of one's actions
I - 12.	FEALTY	L. Need for immediate attention or action
N - 13.	PARTICULAR	M. Object that shows or embodies something
G - 14.	EXPEL	N. Specific; a certain one
Q - 15.	EMBARRASSED	O. Caused to be incapable of movement
V - 16.	PRECIOUS	P. Concentrated; thorough
C - 17.	DELIGHTED	Q. To feel self-conscious or ill at ease
O - 18.	PARALYZED	R. Violent or aggressive; ferocious
S - 19.	HOODLUM	S. Tough and aggressive young man
L - 20.	URGENCY	T. Punishment of being kept in school after hours
U - 21.	CORROSIVE	U. Capable of destroying slowly by chemical action
X - 22.	ABERRATION	V. Valuable; having great value
W - 23.	POSSESSED	W. Controlled as if by a spirit or other force
F - 24.	OBNOXIOUS	X. Unwelcome deviation from normal
J - 25.	FRANTIC	Y. An original model

Freak the Mighty Vocabulary Matching 2

___ 1. ABDUCT   A. Need for immediate attention or action
___ 2. OBLIGATION   B. Nickname
___ 3. PHONY   C. Duty
___ 4. OATH   D. Take (someone) away illegally by force or deception
___ 5. PERSPECTIVE   E. Lacking knowledge
___ 6. PARALYZED   F. Word or phrase communicating an idea
___ 7. SOBRIQUET   G. A view or outlook
___ 8. AUTOMATIC   H. Most favorable; best
___ 9. FRANTIC   I. Valuable; having great value
___10. EXPEL   J. Run hurriedly with short, quick steps
___11. CORROSIVE   K. Protective coloring or disguise
___12. IGNORANT   L. Not operating normally or properly
___13. URGENCY   M. Capable of destroying slowly by chemical action
___14. EMBARRASSED   N. Structure with a square or triangular base and sloping sides that meet in a point at the top
___15. DYSFUNCTIONAL   O. To feel self-conscious or ill at ease
___16. INTENSIVE   P. Caused to be incapable of movement
___17. EXPRESSION   Q. Balanced; made less likely to fall
___18. FUNCTIONAL   R. Fake
___19. OPTIMUM   S. Concentrated; thorough
___20. STABILIZED   T. Eject forcefully
___21. PRECIOUS   U. Solemn promise
___22. CAMOUFLAGE   V. Working by itself with little or no direct human control
___23. STEED   W. Useful; practical; working
___24. SCUTTLE   X. Horse
___25. PYRAMID   Y. Conducted in a hurried and chaotic way; full of fear or anxiety

Freak the Mighty Vocabulary Matching 2 Answer Key

D - 1. ABDUCT	A.	Need for immediate attention or action
C - 2. OBLIGATION	B.	Nickname
R - 3. PHONY	C.	Duty
U - 4. OATH	D.	Take (someone) away illegally by force or deception
G - 5. PERSPECTIVE	E.	Lacking knowledge
P - 6. PARALYZED	F.	Word or phrase communicating an idea
B - 7. SOBRIQUET	G.	A view or outlook
V - 8. AUTOMATIC	H.	Most favorable; best
Y - 9. FRANTIC	I.	Valuable; having great value
T - 10. EXPEL	J.	Run hurriedly with short, quick steps
M - 11. CORROSIVE	K.	Protective coloring or disguise
E - 12. IGNORANT	L.	Not operating normally or properly
A - 13. URGENCY	M.	Capable of destroying slowly by chemical action
O - 14. EMBARRASSED	N.	Structure with a square or triangular base and sloping sides that meet in a point at the top
L - 15. DYSFUNCTIONAL	O.	To feel self-conscious or ill at ease
S - 16. INTENSIVE	P.	Caused to be incapable of movement
F - 17. EXPRESSION	Q.	Balanced; made less likely to fall
W - 18. FUNCTIONAL	R.	Fake
H - 19. OPTIMUM	S.	Concentrated; thorough
Q - 20. STABILIZED	T.	Eject forcefully
I - 21. PRECIOUS	U.	Solemn promise
K - 22. CAMOUFLAGE	V.	Working by itself with little or no direct human control
X - 23. STEED	W.	Useful; practical; working
J - 24. SCUTTLE	X.	Horse
N - 25. PYRAMID	Y.	Conducted in a hurried and chaotic way; full of fear or anxiety

Freak the Mighty Vocabulary Matching 3

___ 1. ESPECIALLY   A. Working by itself with little or no direct human control
___ 2. INVENTION   B. To a great degree; very much
___ 3. OPTIMUM   C. Specific; a certain one
___ 4. MIRACULOUS   D. Structure with a square or triangular base and sloping sides that meet in a point at the top
___ 5. RETRIEVAL   E. Fake
___ 6. EVASIVE   F. Something newly created
___ 7. PRODIGY   G. Unwelcome deviation from normal
___ 8. INJUSTICE   H. Very happy
___ 9. PYRAMID   I. Balanced; made less likely to fall
___ 10. DETENTION   J. Punishment of being kept in school after hours
___ 11. STEED   K. Horse
___ 12. DELIGHTED   L. A view or outlook
___ 13. AUTOMATIC   M. Put into a trance
___ 14. REGURGITATE   N. To vomit
___ 15. SOBRIQUET   O. Something unfair and wrong
___ 16. PARTICULAR   P. Tending or intended to avoid
___ 17. PHONY   Q. Young person with exceptional abilities
___ 18. ACCOMMODATIONS   R. Tied up
___ 19. EXPRESSION   S. Nickname
___ 20. OBLIGATION   T. Duty
___ 21. PERSPECTIVE   U. Word or phrase communicating an idea
___ 22. TRUSSED   V. Living space; lodgings
___ 23. ABERRATION   W. Like a miracle; happening without any natural or scientific explanation
___ 24. STABILIZED   X. Act or process of getting something back
___ 25. HYPNOTIZED   Y. Most favorable; best

Freak the Mighty Vocabulary Matching 3 Answer Key

B - 1. ESPECIALLY
F - 2. INVENTION
Y - 3. OPTIMUM
W - 4. MIRACULOUS
X - 5. RETRIEVAL
P - 6. EVASIVE
Q - 7. PRODIGY
O - 8. INJUSTICE
D - 9. PYRAMID
J - 10. DETENTION
K - 11. STEED
H - 12. DELIGHTED
A - 13. AUTOMATIC
N - 14. REGURGITATE
S - 15. SOBRIQUET
C - 16. PARTICULAR
E - 17. PHONY
V - 18. ACCOMMODATIONS
U - 19. EXPRESSION
T - 20. OBLIGATION
L - 21. PERSPECTIVE
R - 22. TRUSSED
G - 23. ABERRATION
I - 24. STABILIZED
M - 25. HYPNOTIZED

A. Working by itself with little or no direct human control
B. To a great degree; very much
C. Specific; a certain one
D. Structure with a square or triangular base and sloping sides that meet in a point at the top
E. Fake
F. Something newly created
G. Unwelcome deviation from normal
H. Very happy
I. Balanced; made less likely to fall
J. Punishment of being kept in school after hours
K. Horse
L. A view or outlook
M. Put into a trance
N. To vomit
O. Something unfair and wrong
P. Tending or intended to avoid
Q. Young person with exceptional abilities
R. Tied up
S. Nickname
T. Duty
U. Word or phrase communicating an idea
V. Living space; lodgings
W. Like a miracle; happening without any natural or scientific explanation
X. Act or process of getting something back
Y. Most favorable; best

Freak the Mighty Vocabulary Matching 4

___ 1. PROPULSION   A. Valuable; having great value
___ 2. SOBRIQUET   B. Force that sends forward
___ 3. PRECAUTION   C. Violent or aggressive; ferocious
___ 4. OATH   D. Nickname
___ 5. IGNORANT   E. Having difficulty interpreting words, letters, and symbols
___ 6. TRUSSED   F. Balanced; made less likely to fall
___ 7. EXPEL   G. Measure taken in advance to prevent something undesirable from happening
___ 8. ABERRATION   H. Very happy
___ 9. FACILITATE   I. Eject forcefully
___10. FURROWED   J. Stupid person
___11. STABILIZED   K. Living space; lodgings
___12. DELIGHTED   L. Run hurriedly with short, quick steps
___13. CAMOUFLAGE   M. Make easier
___14. MORON   N. The way a person behaves
___15. DYSLEXIC   O. Useful; practical; working
___16. FUNCTIONAL   P. Trenched; rutted; grooved; wrinkled
___17. DEMEANOR   Q. Tied up
___18. ABDUCT   R. Protective coloring or disguise
___19. RETRIEVAL   S. Solemn promise
___20. PRECIOUS   T. Lacking knowledge
___21. PYRAMID   U. Structure with a square or triangular base and sloping sides that meet in a point at the top
___22. ACCOMMODATIONS   V. Punishment of being kept in school after hours
___23. DETENTION   W. Unwelcome deviation from normal
___24. FIERCE   X. Take (someone) away illegally by force or deception
___25. SCUTTLE   Y. Act or process of getting something back

Freak the Mighty Vocabulary Matching 4 Answer Key

B - 1.	PROPULSION	A. Valuable; having great value
D - 2.	SOBRIQUET	B. Force that sends forward
G - 3.	PRECAUTION	C. Violent or aggressive; ferocious
S - 4.	OATH	D. Nickname
T - 5.	IGNORANT	E. Having difficulty interpreting words, letters, and symbols
Q - 6.	TRUSSED	F. Balanced; made less likely to fall
I - 7.	EXPEL	G. Measure taken in advance to prevent something undesirable from happening
W - 8.	ABERRATION	H. Very happy
M - 9.	FACILITATE	I. Eject forcefully
P - 10.	FURROWED	J. Stupid person
F - 11.	STABILIZED	K. Living space; lodgings
H - 12.	DELIGHTED	L. Run hurriedly with short, quick steps
R - 13.	CAMOUFLAGE	M. Make easier
J - 14.	MORON	N. The way a person behaves
E - 15.	DYSLEXIC	O. Useful; practical; working
O - 16.	FUNCTIONAL	P. Trenched; rutted; grooved; wrinkled
N - 17.	DEMEANOR	Q. Tied up
X - 18.	ABDUCT	R. Protective coloring or disguise
Y - 19.	RETRIEVAL	S. Solemn promise
A - 20.	PRECIOUS	T. Lacking knowledge
U - 21.	PYRAMID	U. Structure with a square or triangular base and sloping sides that meet in a point at the top
K - 22.	ACCOMMODATIONS	V. Punishment of being kept in school after hours
V - 23.	DETENTION	W. Unwelcome deviation from normal
C - 24.	FIERCE	X. Take (someone) away illegally by force or deception
L - 25.	SCUTTLE	Y. Act or process of getting something back

Freak the Mighty Vocabulary Magic Squares 1

Match the definition with the vocabulary word. Put your answers in the magic squares below. When your answers are correct, all columns and rows will add to the same number.

A. SOBRIQUET
B. STEED
C. TEMPORARY
D. PRECIOUS
E. OPTIMUM
F. REGURGITATE
G. VIOLATE
H. MORON
I. ACCOMMODATIONS
J. IGNORANT
K. INTENSIVE
L. MIRACULOUS
M. DYSFUNCTIONAL
N. TROUSERS
O. TRUSSED
P. URGENCY

1. Nickname
2. Pants
3. Lacking knowledge
4. Most favorable; best
5. Break or fail to comply with a rule or agreement
6. Like a miracle; happening without any natural or scientific explanation
7. Need for immediate attention or action
8. Not lasting
9. Tied up
10. Valuable; having great value
11. Stupid person
12. Concentrated; thorough
13. Living space; lodgings
14. To vomit
15. Horse
16. Not operating normally or properly

A=	B=	C=	D=
E=	F=	G=	H=
I=	J=	K=	L=
M=	N=	O=	P=

Freak the Mighty Vocabulary Magic Squares 1 Answer Key

Match the definition with the vocabulary word. Put your answers in the magic squares below. When your answers are correct, all columns and rows will add to the same number.

A. SOBRIQUET
B. STEED
C. TEMPORARY
D. PRECIOUS
E. OPTIMUM
F. REGURGITATE
G. VIOLATE
H. MORON
I. ACCOMMODATIONS
J. IGNORANT
K. INTENSIVE
L. MIRACULOUS
M. DYSFUNCTIONAL
N. TROUSERS
O. TRUSSED
P. URGENCY

1. Nickname
2. Pants
3. Lacking knowledge
4. Most favorable; best
5. Break or fail to comply with a rule or agreement
6. Like a miracle; happening without any natural or scientific explanation
7. Need for immediate attention or action
8. Not lasting
9. Tied up
10. Valuable; having great value
11. Stupid person
12. Concentrated; thorough
13. Living space; lodgings
14. To vomit
15. Horse
16. Not operating normally or properly

A=1	B=15	C=8	D=10
E=4	F=14	G=5	H=11
I=13	J=3	K=12	L=6
M=16	N=2	O=9	P=7

Freak the Mighty Vocabulary Magic Squares 2

Match the definition with the vocabulary word. Put your answers in the magic squares below. When your answers are correct, all columns and rows will add to the same number.

A. DETENTION
B. ACCOMMODATIONS
C. PRECAUTION
D. CORROSIVE
E. INTENSIVE
F. MIRACULOUS
G. CONSEQUENCES
H. INJUSTICE
I. TRUSSED
J. FURROWED
K. ABERRATION
L. FUNCTIONAL
M. TENEMENTS
N. HOODLUM
O. TRACHEOTOMY
P. OBLIGATION

1. Incision in the windpipe made to relieve an obstruction to breathing
2. Capable of destroying slowly by chemical action
3. Trenched; rutted; grooved; wrinkled
4. Concentrated; thorough
5. Tied up
6. Like a miracle; happening without any natural or scientific explanation
7. Duty
8. Measure taken in advance to prevent something undesirable from happening
9. Something unfair and wrong
10. Unwelcome deviation from normal
11. Punishment of being kept in school after hours
12. Tough and aggressive young man
13. Living space; lodgings
14. Apartment houses over-crowded and poorly maintained
15. Results of one's actions
16. Useful; practical; working

A=	B=	C=	D=
E=	F=	G=	H=
I=	J=	K=	L=
M=	N=	O=	P=

Freak the Mighty Vocabulary Magic Squares 2 Answer Key

Match the definition with the vocabulary word. Put your answers in the magic squares below. When your answers are correct, all columns and rows will add to the same number.

A. DETENTION
B. ACCOMMODATIONS
C. PRECAUTION
D. CORROSIVE
E. INTENSIVE
F. MIRACULOUS
G. CONSEQUENCES
H. INJUSTICE
I. TRUSSED
J. FURROWED
K. ABERRATION
L. FUNCTIONAL
M. TENEMENTS
N. HOODLUM
O. TRACHEOTOMY
P. OBLIGATION

1. Incision in the windpipe made to relieve an obstruction to breathing
2. Capable of destroying slowly by chemical action
3. Trenched; rutted; grooved; wrinkled
4. Concentrated; thorough
5. Tied up
6. Like a miracle; happening without any natural or scientific explanation
7. Duty
8. Measure taken in advance to prevent something undesirable from happening
9. Something unfair and wrong
10. Unwelcome deviation from normal
11. Punishment of being kept in school after hours
12. Tough and aggressive young man
13. Living space; lodgings
14. Apartment houses over-crowded and poorly maintained
15. Results of one's actions
16. Useful; practical; working

A=11	B=13	C=8	D=2
E=4	F=6	G=15	H=9
I=5	J=3	K=10	L=16
M=14	N=12	O=1	P=7

Freak the Mighty Vocabulary Magic Squares 3

Match the definition with the vocabulary word. Put your answers in the magic squares below. When your answers are correct, all columns and rows will add to the same number.

A. TRUSSED
B. MIRACULOUS
C. TRACHEOTOMY
D. PRECAUTION
E. DYSLEXIC
F. MANIFESTATION
G. OBLIGATION
H. INTENSIVE
I. OBNOXIOUS
J. URGENCY
K. REGURGITATE
L. EMBARRASSED
M. PRODIGY
N. PHONY
O. CAMOUFLAGE
P. STEED

1. Concentrated; thorough
2. Young person with exceptional abilities
3. Like a miracle; happening without any natural or scientific explanation
4. To vomit
5. Need for immediate attention or action
6. Incision in the windpipe made to relieve an obstruction to breathing
7. Horse
8. Having difficulty interpreting words, letters, and symbols
9. Protective coloring or disguise
10. Object that shows or embodies something
11. Extremely unpleasant
12. Measure taken in advance to prevent something undesirable from happening
13. Tied up
14. To feel self-conscious or ill at ease
15. Duty
16. Fake

A=	B=	C=	D=
E=	F=	G=	H=
I=	J=	K=	L=
M=	N=	O=	P=

Freak the Mighty Vocabulary Magic Squares 3 Answer Key

Match the definition with the vocabulary word. Put your answers in the magic squares below. When your answers are correct, all columns and rows will add to the same number.

A. TRUSSED
B. MIRACULOUS
C. TRACHEOTOMY
D. PRECAUTION
E. DYSLEXIC
F. MANIFESTATION
G. OBLIGATION
H. INTENSIVE
I. OBNOXIOUS
J. URGENCY
K. REGURGITATE
L. EMBARRASSED
M. PRODIGY
N. PHONY
O. CAMOUFLAGE
P. STEED

1. Concentrated; thorough
2. Young person with exceptional abilities
3. Like a miracle; happening without any natural or scientific explanation
4. To vomit
5. Need for immediate attention or action
6. Incision in the windpipe made to relieve an obstruction to breathing
7. Horse
8. Having difficulty interpreting words, letters, and symbols
9. Protective coloring or disguise
10. Object that shows or embodies something
11. Extremely unpleasant
12. Measure taken in advance to prevent something undesirable from happening
13. Tied up
14. To feel self-conscious or ill at ease
15. Duty
16. Fake

A=13	B=3	C=6	D=12
E=8	F=10	G=15	H=1
I=11	J=5	K=4	L=14
M=2	N=16	O=9	P=7

Freak the Mighty Vocabulary Magic Squares 4

Match the definition with the vocabulary word. Put your answers in the magic squares below. When your answers are correct, all columns and rows will add to the same number.

A. EMBARRASSED
B. PHONY
C. FIERCE
D. INJUSTICE
E. INVENTION
F. TRACHEOTOMY
G. ESPECIALLY
H. OATH
I. FRANTIC
J. PRODIGY
K. SCUTTLE
L. FACILITATE
M. IGNORANT
N. PRECIOUS
O. STABILIZED
P. FEALTY

1. Fake
2. To a great degree; very much
3. Run hurriedly with short, quick steps
4. Valuable; having great value
5. Lacking knowledge
6. Make easier
7. Solemn promise
8. To feel self-conscious or ill at ease
9. Loyalty; faithfulness
10. Conducted in a hurried and chaotic way; full of fear or anxiety
11. Something newly created
12. Something unfair and wrong
13. Violent or aggressive; ferocious
14. Incision in the windpipe made to relieve an obstruction to breathing
15. Young person with exceptional abilities
16. Balanced; made less likely to fall

A=	B=	C=	D=
E=	F=	G=	H=
I=	J=	K=	L=
M=	N=	O=	P=

Freak the Mighty Vocabulary Magic Squares 4 Answer Key

Match the definition with the vocabulary word. Put your answers in the magic squares below. When your answers are correct, all columns and rows will add to the same number.

A. EMBARRASSED
B. PHONY
C. FIERCE
D. INJUSTICE
E. INVENTION
F. TRACHEOTOMY
G. ESPECIALLY
H. OATH
I. FRANTIC
J. PRODIGY
K. SCUTTLE
L. FACILITATE
M. IGNORANT
N. PRECIOUS
O. STABILIZED
P. FEALTY

1. Fake
2. To a great degree; very much
3. Run hurriedly with short, quick steps
4. Valuable; having great value
5. Lacking knowledge
6. Make easier
7. Solemn promise
8. To feel self-conscious or ill at ease
9. Loyalty; faithfulness
10. Conducted in a hurried and chaotic way; full of fear or anxiety
11. Something newly created
12. Something unfair and wrong
13. Violent or aggressive; ferocious
14. Incision in the windpipe made to relieve an obstruction to breathing
15. Young person with exceptional abilities
16. Balanced; made less likely to fall

A=8	B=1	C=13	D=12
E=11	F=14	G=2	H=7
I=10	J=15	K=3	L=6
M=5	N=4	O=16	P=9

Freak the Mighty Vocabulary Word Search 1

```
D P A R T I C U L A R U P S D F Y A P
I Y V I O L A T E L C R Z T E R R R O
V E S P E C I A L L Y G C A M A O C S
U K Z F U R R O W E D E O B E N T H S
L A B D U C T E Z S M N N I A T C E E
G S B Z T N Z K G Q L C V L N I E T S
E O P P R E C I O U S Y E I O C J Y S
D B P F E A L T Y H R T R Z R N A P E
E R N T S I F X I N R G G E F Y R E D
L I O T I T N A R O N G I D O A T H Y
I Q B E T M V T U I N F N T D K Y R L
G U N N C P U S E T D A G Q A G Y A Y
H E O E G G E M Q N R E L K I T V W V
T T X M O R O N B E S N T D D E E T S
E V I E S P K T G V F I O E I X V Y Q
D D O N T Q P N N R H R V R N T A P Q
B F U T L X I H K E P H T E X T S N Z
D E S S U R T G O T L E J E U Q I N U
I N J U S T I C E N R Z J P P C V O T
C O R R O S I V E I Y E X P E L E R N
```

ABDUCT	EXPEL	OATH	SOBRIQUET
ARCHETYPE	FEALTY	OBNOXIOUS	STABILIZED
CONVERGING	FIERCE	OPTIMUM	STEED
CORROSIVE	FRANTIC	PARTICULAR	TENEMENTS
DELIGHTED	FUNCTIONAL	PHONY	TRAJECTORY
DEMEANOR	FURROWED	POSSESSED	TROUSERS
DETENTION	IGNORANT	PRECIOUS	TRUSSED
DIVULGED	INJUSTICE	PRODIGY	UNIQUE
DYSFUNCTIONAL	INTENSIVE	REGURGITATE	URGENCY
ESPECIALLY	INTERVENTION	RETRIEVAL	VIOLATE
EVASIVE	MORON	RINGER	

Freak the Mighty Vocabulary Word Search 1 Answer Key

```
D P A R T I C U L A R   U   S D F Y A P
I Y V I O L A T E       R   T E R R C O
V E S P E C I A L L Y   G C A M O H S
U   F U R R O W E D     E C B E N T E
L A B D U C T E         N O I A I C S
G S     N       G       C N L N   E S
E O   P R E C I O U S   Y E I O   J E
D B P F E A L T Y       R R Z R   A P D
  R   T I         N     R G E D   R   
L I O T T N A R O N G   G I D   O T   
I Q B E   M   T U I N   F N T       Y L
G U N N     U S E T D   A G   A   G A
H E O E     E M N R E   L     I   T V
T T X M O R O N   E S   T D D E   E T S
E   I E S       G V     I O E I   V
D   O N     P N   R     O R N A   A
    U T     I H   E P   T   E T   S
D E S S U R T   O T     E   E U Q I N U
I N J U S T I C E N R               V O
C O R R O S I V E I Y E X P E L E     N
```

ABDUCT EXPEL OATH SOBRIQUET

ARCHETYPE FEALTY OBNOXIOUS STABILIZED

CONVERGING FIERCE OPTIMUM STEED

CORROSIVE FRANTIC PARTICULAR TENEMENTS

DELIGHTED FUNCTIONAL PHONY TRAJECTORY

DEMEANOR FURROWED POSSESSED TROUSERS

DETENTION IGNORANT PRECIOUS TRUSSED

DIVULGED INJUSTICE PRODIGY UNIQUE

DYSFUNCTIONAL INTENSIVE REGURGITATE URGENCY

ESPECIALLY INTERVENTION RETRIEVAL VIOLATE

EVASIVE MORON RINGER

Freak the Mighty Vocabulary Word Search 2

```
E V A S I V E H P Y R A M I D S C C T
Y I P Z D F X D O D F R A N T I C O R
X O M R E D G A I O B X Y Y T R E N A
C L L A O Y D V B Q D B B A A L S S J
S A B M D U X V D H L M L K M P E E
E T A T I L I C A F U O U Y B S E Q C
Y E E D G A G G L W T C N M O C C U T
L P R E X N M H Y U I O T B R Y I E O
M R D M D O B I A T H N R E L U A N R
H O I E M I H Z R P S I I E N E L C Y
O P N A P T N A C A Q F P I M M L E E
B U V N A C P T H U C X Q Z Y B Y S X
N L E O R N U W E K E U R M B A G T P
O S N R A U R T T N E Z L M O R O N R
X I T I L F G R Y N S X W O R R Q E E
I O I N Y S E U P T P I G V U A J M S
O N O G Z Y N S E G Q M V W C S L E S
U Z N E E D C S C U T T L E J S L N I
S W N R D H Y E P O S S E S S E D E O
C I X E L S Y D E W O R R U F D S T N
```

ABDUCT
ARCHETYPE
AUTOMATIC
CONSEQUENCES
DEMEANOR
DIVULGED
DYSFUNCTIONAL
DYSLEXIC
EMBARRASSED
ESPECIALLY
EVASIVE

EXPEL
EXPRESSION
FACILITATE
FEALTY
FIERCE
FRANTIC
FURROWED
HOODLUM
INTENSIVE
INVENTION
MIRACULOUS

MORON
OATH
OBNOXIOUS
PARALYZED
PARTICULAR
PHONY
POSSESSED
PRODIGY
PROPULSION
PYRAMID
RINGER

SCUTTLE
SOBRIQUET
STEED
TENEMENTS
TRAJECTORY
TRUSSED
UNIQUE
URGENCY
VIOLATE

Freak the Mighty Vocabulary Word Search 2 Answer Key

```
E   V   A   S   I   V   E   H       P   Y   R   A   M   I   D       C   C   T
    I   P       F           O   D   F   R   A   N   T   I       C   O   R
    O       R   E           A   I   O               T       R   E   N   A
    L       A   O       V   B       D           A   A           S   S   J
S   A           D           D       L   M       L               P   E   E
E   T   A   T   I   L   I   C   A   F   U   O   U   Y           S   Q   C
Y   E       D   G   A       G       T   C   N   M       O       C   U   T
    P           E       N   M       Y   I   O   T   B       R   I   E   O
    R       D   M   D   O       I   A   T   H   R   E   L   U   A   N   R
    O           I   E       I   H       R   P       I   I   E   N   L   C   Y
O   P   N       A   P   T   N   A   C   A   Q   F   P   I       M       E
B   U   V       N   A   C   P   T   H   U   C   X   Q           B   Y   S
N   L   E       O   R   N   U       E       U           L       A       T
O   S   N       R   A   U   R   T   T   N   E       M   O   R   O   N   R
X   I   T       I   L   F   G   R   Y           S       O       R       E
I   O   I       N   Y   S   E   U   P                   I   U   A       M   S
O   N   O       G   Z   Y   N   S           I           V       S   E   S
U       N       F   F   D   C   S   C   U   T   T   L   E       S   N   I
S       R           D       Y   E   P   O   S   S   E   S   S   E   D   E
C   I   X   E   L   S   Y   D   E   W   O   R   R   U   F       D       T   N
```

ABDUCT	EXPEL	MORON	SCUTTLE
ARCHETYPE	EXPRESSION	OATH	SOBRIQUET
AUTOMATIC	FACILITATE	OBNOXIOUS	STEED
CONSEQUENCES	FEALTY	PARALYZED	TENEMENTS
DEMEANOR	FIERCE	PARTICULAR	TRAJECTORY
DIVULGED	FRANTIC	PHONY	TRUSSED
DYSFUNCTIONAL	FURROWED	POSSESSED	UNIQUE
DYSLEXIC	HOODLUM	PRODIGY	URGENCY
EMBARRASSED	INTENSIVE	PROPULSION	VIOLATE
ESPECIALLY	INVENTION	PYRAMID	
EVASIVE	MIRACULOUS	RINGER	

Freak the Mighty Vocabulary Word Search 3

```
H N H Y S E X P E L Q S B Q S M D M E
Y O D Y R T E M E L E T R W E U D X V
P I Q N D E W O R R U F O T C L E C A
N S M O J M J V T C S L N G R D G X S
O S U H J O O P O Q S P A R E O L Y I
T E M P O R A R Y U P R E C I O U S V
I R I V P C R T O R L M M C F H V C E
Z P T X G O N I H N A C E M T V I O D
E X P H S L X V C R T M D S T I D N Y
D E O I V O P I K N Q Y I N Z O V S S
E Z V G N N T A P O G V A D G L G E F
E E P B L A B Y W I R R E Y N A P Q U
T F O C M L F K D T O S X C I T T U N
S S V O E M C O F N S R I N G E R E C
Z C T K U J R B G E J F Y E R S O N T
C U P S Q P B I S T A W T G E F U C I
A T Y V I T W S S E H L J R V P S E O
S T X X N Q O A B D U C T U N Z E S N
S L J R U P T R U S S E D Y O J R Y A
D E S N O I T A D O M M O C C A S X L
```

A view or outlook (11)
Break or fail to comply with a rule or agreement (7)
Capable of destroying slowly by chemical action (9)
Coming together in one place (10)
Controlled as if by a spirit or other force (9)
Eject forcefully (5)
Extremely unpleasant (9)
Fake (5)
Horse (5)
Informal term for a person's double (6)
Lacking knowledge (8)
Living space; lodgings (14)
Loyalty; faithfulness (6)
Made known; revealed (8)
Most favorable; best (7)
Need for immediate attention or action (7)
Not lasting (9)
Not operating normally or properly (13)
One of a kind (6)
Pants (8)
Punishment of being kept in school after hours (9)
Put into a trance (10)
Results of one's actions (12)
Run hurriedly with short, quick steps (7)
Stupid person (5)
Solemn promise (4)
Structure with a square or triangular base and sloping sides that meet in a point at the top (7)
Take (someone) away illegally by force or deception (6)
Tending or intended to avoid (7)
The way a person behaves (8)
Tied up (7)
Tough and aggressive young man (7)
Transmission of readings to a distant receiving set or station (9)
Trenched; rutted; grooved; wrinkled (8)
Uncommon; worthy of notice (10)
Valuable; having great value (8)
Violent or aggressive; ferocious (6)
Word or phrase communicating an idea (10)
Working by itself with little or no direct human control (9)
Young person with exceptional abilities (7)

Freak the Mighty Vocabulary Word Search 3 Answer Key

[word search grid omitted]

A view or outlook (11)
Break or fail to comply with a rule or agreement (7)
Capable of destroying slowly by chemical action (9)
Coming together in one place (10)
Controlled as if by a spirit or other force (9)
Eject forcefully (5)
Extremely unpleasant (9)
Fake (5)
Horse (5)
Informal term for a person's double (6)
Lacking knowledge (8)
Living space; lodgings (14)
Loyalty; faithfulness (6)
Made known; revealed (8)
Most favorable; best (7)
Need for immediate attention or action (7)
Not lasting (9)
Not operating normally or properly (13)
One of a kind (6)
Pants (8)
Punishment of being kept in school after hours (9)
Put into a trance (10)
Results of one's actions (12)
Run hurriedly with short, quick steps (7)
Stupid person (5)
Solemn promise (4)
Structure with a square or triangular base and sloping sides that meet in a point at the top (7)
Take (someone) away illegally by force or deception (6)
Tending or intended to avoid (7)
The way a person behaves (8)
Tied up (7)
Tough and aggressive young man (7)
Transmission of readings to a distant receiving set or station (9)
Trenched; rutted; grooved; wrinkled (8)
Uncommon; worthy of notice (10)
Valuable; having great value (8)
Violent or aggressive; ferocious (6)
Word or phrase communicating an idea (10)
Working by itself with little or no direct human control (9)
Young person with exceptional abilities (7)

Freak the Mighty Vocabulary Word Search 4

```
I C A M O U F L A G E P R E C I O U S
N I B Q P P E A R R B V T N P X L G T
T T E K T S A S C J I A A B R A K D A
E A R F I W L R N I T N S S V S T N B
N M R E M R T Q A I L T G E I E E V I
S O A V U R Y D G L P I I E P V L P L
I T T I M B E R I N Y R T Y R V E O I
V U I S P W U M O N T Z T A E V M S Z
E A O O O G T I A E J E E M T D E S E
F V N R E F T R R R H U Q D A E T E D
F U R R Y U B H U C K X S H L N R S G
T U N O A F R T R S B A V T O J Y S D
F D T C I T N A R F S O B R I Q U E T
U J E E T A B O B R J E O L V C L D M
Q R R M R I C F E D T M D P E I E U C
P C G O E L O S M S U K V B G N L N B
E H N E E A U N Z Y T C B H B D V I L
T G O P N O N F A B K E T X O P F Q S
I Q X N R C T O Q L W E E O B B H U S
B E K T Y T Y J R B D R H D S J V E H
```

Act or process of getting something back (9)
An original model (9)
Balanced; made less likely to fall (10)
Break or fail to comply with a rule or agreement (7)
Capable of destroying slowly by chemical action (9)
Caused to be incapable of movement (9)
Concentrated; thorough (9)
Conducted in a hurried and chaotic way; full of fear or anxiety (7)
Controlled as if by a spirit or other force (9)
Eject forcefully (5)
Fake (5)
Horse (5)
Informal term for a person's double (6)
Lacking knowledge (8)
Loyalty; faithfulness (6)
Make easier (10)
Measure taken in advance to prevent something undesirable from happening (10)
Most favorable; best (7)
Need for immediate attention or action (7)
Nickname (9)

One of a kind (6)
Pants (8)
Protective coloring or disguise (10)
Stupid person (5)
Solemn promise (4)
Something unfair and wrong (9)
Take (someone) away illegally by force or deception (6)
Tending or intended to avoid (7)
The way a person behaves (8)
Tied up (7)
To vomit (11)
Tough and aggressive young man (7)
Transmission of readings to a distant receiving set or station (9)
Trenched; rutted; grooved; wrinkled (8)
Uncommon; worthy of notice (10)
Unwelcome deviation from normal (10)
Useful; practical; working (10)
Valuable; having great value (8)
Very happy (9)
Violent or aggressive; ferocious (6)
Working by itself with little or no direct human control (9)

Freak the Mighty Vocabulary Word Search 4 Answer Key

Act or process of getting something back (9)
An original model (9)
Balanced; made less likely to fall (10)
Break or fail to comply with a rule or agreement (7)
Capable of destroying slowly by chemical action (9)
Caused to be incapable of movement (9)
Concentrated; thorough (9)
Conducted in a hurried and chaotic way; full of fear or anxiety (7)
Controlled as if by a spirit or other force (9)
Eject forcefully (5)
Fake (5)
Horse (5)
Informal term for a person's double (6)
Lacking knowledge (8)
Loyalty; faithfulness (6)
Make easier (10)
Measure taken in advance to prevent something undesirable from happening (10)
Most favorable; best (7)
Need for immediate attention or action (7)
Nickname (9)
One of a kind (6)
Pants (8)
Protective coloring or disguise (10)
Stupid person (5)
Solemn promise (4)
Something unfair and wrong (9)
Take (someone) away illegally by force or deception (6)
Tending or intended to avoid (7)
The way a person behaves (8)
Tied up (7)
To vomit (11)
Tough and aggressive young man (7)
Transmission of readings to a distant receiving set or station (9)
Trenched; rutted; grooved; wrinkled (8)
Uncommon; worthy of notice (10)
Unwelcome deviation from normal (10)
Useful; practical; working (10)
Valuable; having great value (8)
Very happy (9)
Violent or aggressive; ferocious (6)
Working by itself with little or no direct human control (9)

Freak the Mighty Vocabulary Crossword 1

Across
1. Conducted in a hurried and chaotic way; full of fear or anxiety
3. The way a person behaves
5. Coming together in one place
8. Run hurriedly with short, quick steps
12. Choices
14. Informal term for a person's double
16. Solemn promise
18. Break or fail to comply with a rule or agreement
19. Lacking knowledge
20. Having difficulty interpreting words, letters, and symbols

Down
2. Take (someone) away illegally by force or deception
4. Stupid person
6. Duty
7. Something newly created
8. Balanced; made less likely to fall
9. Tending or intended to avoid
10. Loyalty; faithfulness
11. Violent or aggressive; ferocious
13. To feel self-conscious or ill at ease
14. To vomit
15. Fake
17. Horse

Freak the Mighty Vocabulary Crossword 1 Answer Key

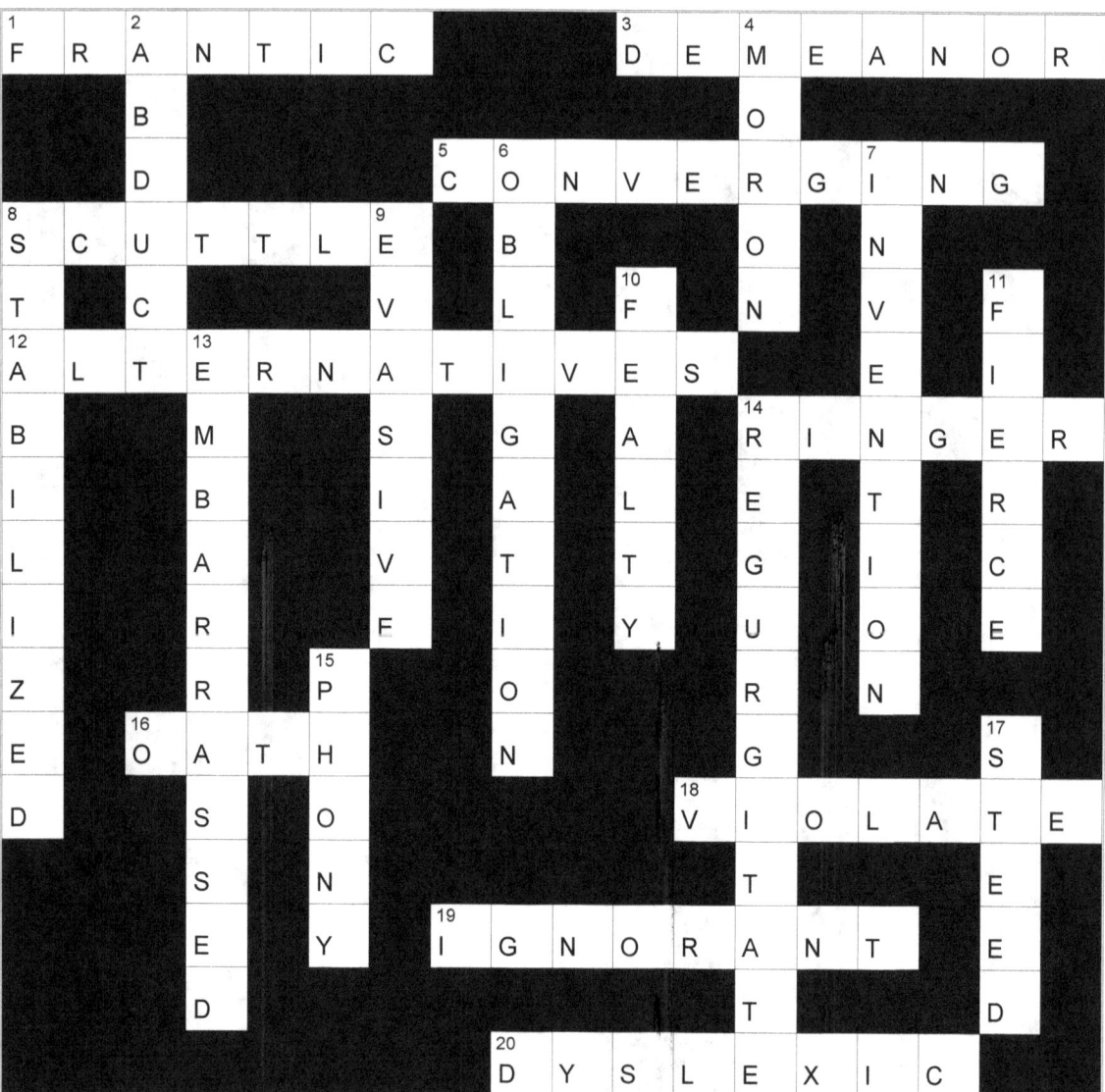

Across
1. Conducted in a hurried and chaotic way; full of fear or anxiety
3. The way a person behaves
5. Coming together in one place
8. Run hurriedly with short, quick steps
12. Choices
14. Informal term for a person's double
16. Solemn promise
18. Break or fail to comply with a rule or agreement
19. Lacking knowledge
20. Having difficulty interpreting words, letters, and symbols

Down
2. Take (someone) away illegally by force or deception
4. Stupid person
6. Duty
7. Something newly created
8. Balanced; made less likely to fall
9. Tending or intended to avoid
10. Loyalty; faithfulness
11. Violent or aggressive; ferocious
13. To feel self-conscious or ill at ease
14. To vomit
15. Fake
17. Horse

Freak the Mighty Vocabulary Crossword 2

Across
1. Working by itself with little or no direct human control
4. Violent or aggressive; ferocious
6. Structure with a square or triangular base and sloping sides that meet in a point at the top
9. Most favorable; best
14. Made known; revealed
15. Solemn promise
16. Horse
17. Informal term for a person's double
18. Conducted in a hurried and chaotic way; full of fear or anxiety
19. Concentrated; thorough

Down
2. Take (someone) away illegally by force or deception
3. Lacking knowledge
5. Protective coloring or disguise
6. Fake
7. Act or process of getting something back
8. Stupid person
10. The path of a moving body or particle
11. Object that shows or embodies something
12. Transmission of readings to a distant receiving set or station
13. Loyalty; faithfulness
14. Punishment of being kept in school after hours

Freak the Mighty Vocabulary Crossword 2 Answer Key

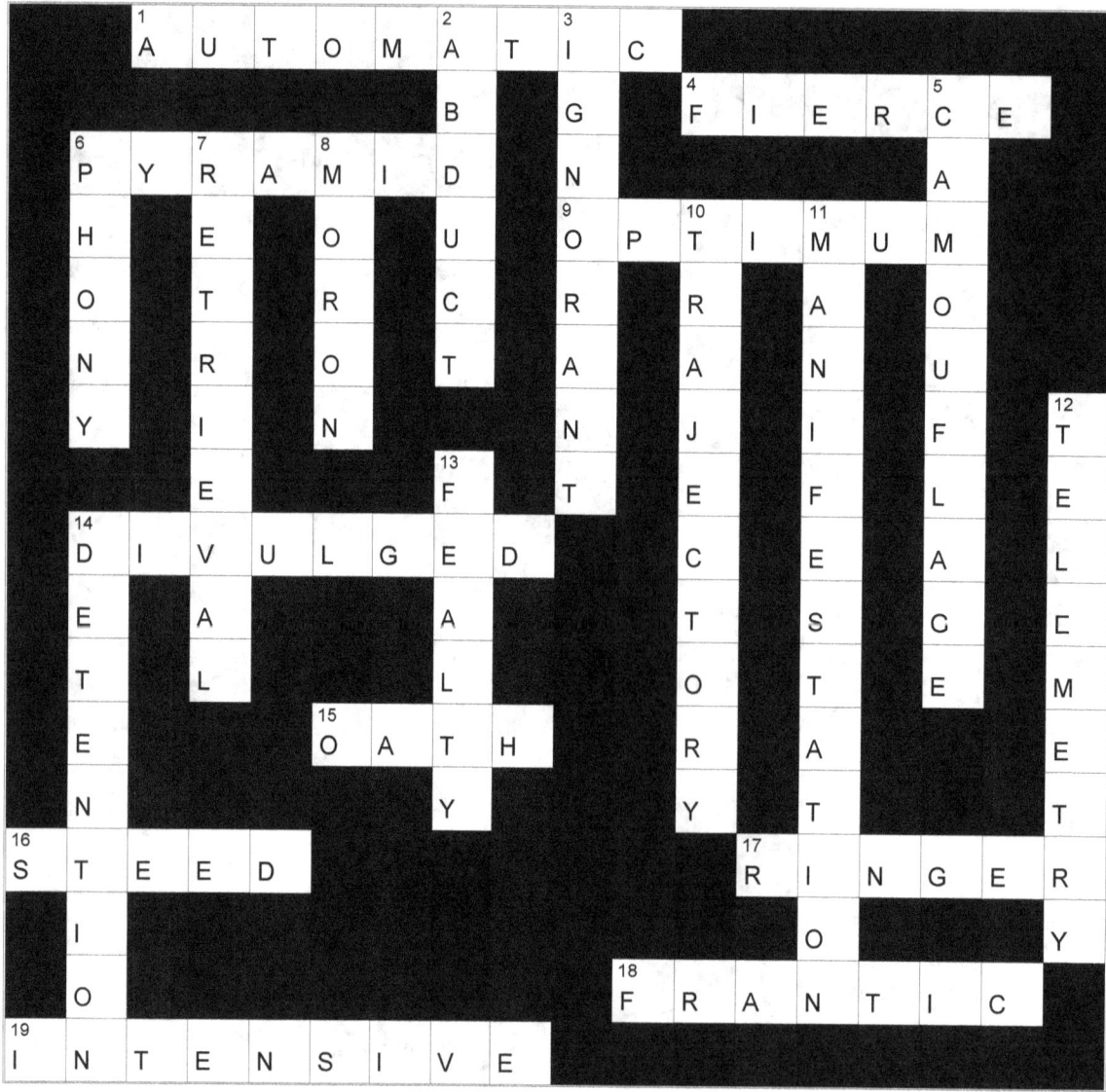

Across
1. Working by itself with little or no direct human control
4. Violent or aggressive; ferocious
6. Structure with a square or triangular base and sloping sides that meet in a point at the top
9. Most favorable; best
14. Made known; revealed
15. Solemn promise
16. Horse
17. Informal term for a person's double
18. Conducted in a hurried and chaotic way; full of fear or anxiety
19. Concentrated; thorough

Down
2. Take (someone) away illegally by force or deception
3. Lacking knowledge
5. Protective coloring or disguise
6. Fake
7. Act or process of getting something back
8. Stupid person
10. The path of a moving body or particle
11. Object that shows or embodies something
12. Transmission of readings to a distant receiving set or station
13. Loyalty; faithfulness
14. Punishment of being kept in school after hours

Freak the Mighty Vocabulary Crossword 3

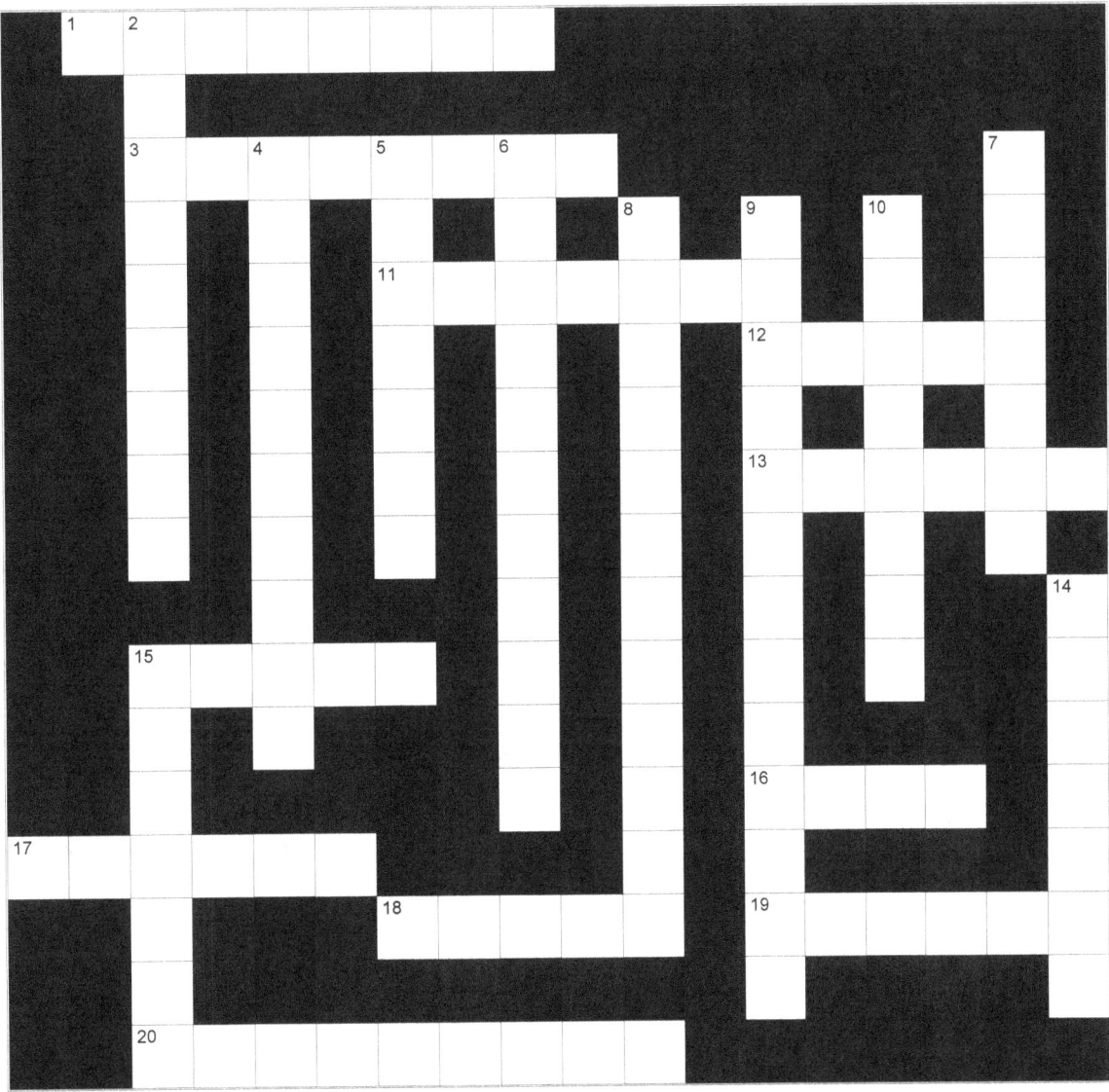

Across
1. Made known; revealed
3. Pants
11. Need for immediate attention or action
12. Horse
13. One of a kind
15. Fake
16. Solemn promise
17. Loyalty; faithfulness
18. Stupid person
19. Take (someone) away illegally by force or deception
20. Punishment of being kept in school after hours

Down
2. Concentrated; thorough
4. Duty
5. Run hurriedly with short, quick steps
6. To vomit
7. Tough and aggressive young man
8. Action taken to improve a medical disorder
9. Not operating normally or properly
10. Valuable; having great value
14. Break or fail to comply with a rule or agreement
15. Structure with a square or triangular base and sloping sides that meet in a point at the top

Freak the Mighty Vocabulary Crossword 3 Answer Key

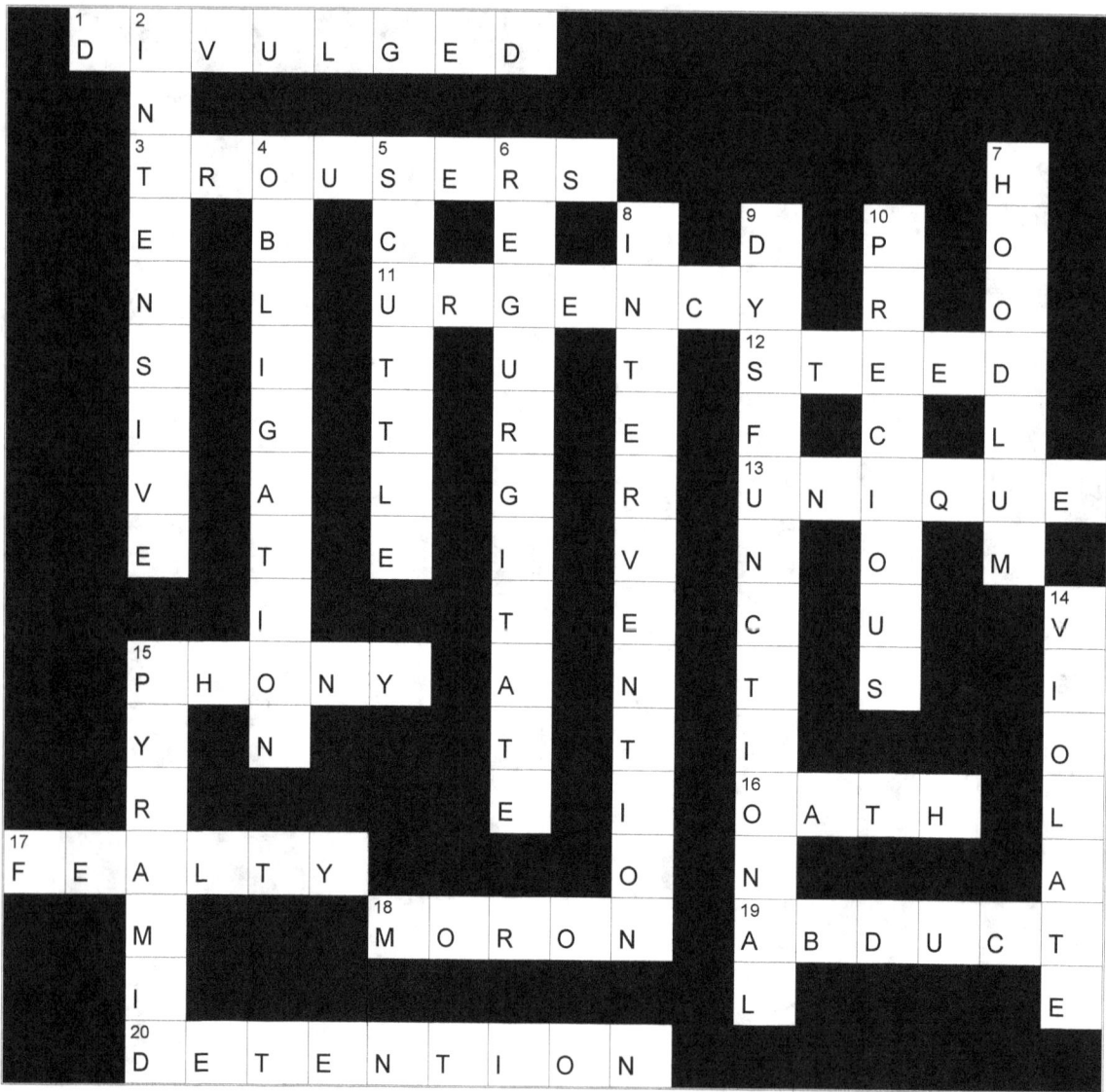

Across
1. Made known; revealed
3. Pants
11. Need for immediate attention or action
12. Horse
13. One of a kind
15. Fake
16. Solemn promise
17. Loyalty; faithfulness
18. Stupid person
19. Take (someone) away illegally by force or deception
20. Punishment of being kept in school after hours

Down
2. Concentrated; thorough
4. Duty
5. Run hurriedly with short, quick steps
6. To vomit
7. Tough and aggressive young man
8. Action taken to improve a medical disorder
9. Not operating normally or properly
10. Valuable; having great value
14. Break or fail to comply with a rule or agreement
15. Structure with a square or triangular base and sloping sides that meet in a point at the top

Freak the Mighty Vocabulary Crossword 4

Across
1. Fake
3. Trenched; rutted; grooved; wrinkled
7. Coming together in one place
8. Loyalty; faithfulness
10. Like a miracle; happening without any natural or scientific explanation
13. Eject forcefully
18. Working by itself with little or no direct human control
19. Run hurriedly with short, quick steps
20. Stupid person
21. Pants

Down
2. Tough and aggressive young man
3. Useful; practical; working
4. Informal term for a person's double
5. To a great degree; very much
6. Need for immediate attention or action
9. Protective coloring or disguise
11. Something newly created
12. Horse
14. Valuable; having great value
15. The way a person behaves
16. Most favorable; best
17. Solemn promise

Freak the Mighty Vocabulary Crossword 4 Answer Key

Across
1. Fake
3. Trenched; rutted; grooved; wrinkled
7. Coming together in one place
8. Loyalty; faithfulness
10. Like a miracle; happening without any natural or scientific explanation
13. Eject forcefully
18. Working by itself with little or no direct human control
19. Run hurriedly with short, quick steps
20. Stupid person
21. Pants

Down
2. Tough and aggressive young man
3. Useful; practical; working
4. Informal term for a person's double
5. To a great degree; very much
6. Need for immediate attention or action
9. Protective coloring or disguise
11. Something newly created
12. Horse
14. Valuable; having great value
15. The way a person behaves
16. Most favorable; best
17. Solemn promise

Freak the Mighty Vocabulary Juggle Letters 1

1. STINIENEV   = 1. _____
   Concentrated; thorough

2. ZATISLBIDE   = 2. _____
   Balanced; made less likely to fall

3. RRNIEG   = 3. _____
   Informal term for a person's double

4. DESTE   = 4. _____
   Horse

5. AAERMBKLER   = 5. _____
   Uncommon; worthy of notice

6. UONOBIOXS   = 6. _____
   Extremely unpleasant

7. YODIPGR   = 7. _____
   Young person with exceptional abilities

8. CDUATB   = 8. _____
   Take (someone) away illegally by force or deception

9. NETSNEETM   = 9. _____
   Apartment houses over-crowded and poorly maintained

10. IESLCELAYP =10. _____
    To a great degree; very much

11. NROMO   =11. _____
    Stupid person

12. SOVORIERC   =12. _____
    Capable of destroying slowly by chemical action

13. UMLRIAUSOC =13. _____
    Like a miracle; happening without any natural or scientific explanation

14. ALDYARPZE   =14. _____
    Caused to be incapable of movement

15. CTPALAURRI =15. _____
    Specific; a certain one

Freak the Mighty Vocabulary Juggle Letters 1 Answer Key

1. STINIENEV = 1. INTENSIVE
   Concentrated; thorough

2. ZATISLBIDE = 2. STABILIZED
   Balanced; made less likely to fall

3. RRNIEG = 3. RINGER
   Informal term for a person's double

4. DESTE = 4. STEED
   Horse

5. AAERMBKLER = 5. REMARKABLE
   Uncommon; worthy of notice

6. UONOBIOXS = 6. OBNOXIOUS
   Extremely unpleasant

7. YODIPGR = 7. PRODIGY
   Young person with exceptional abilities

8. CDUATB = 8. ABDUCT
   Take (someone) away illegally by force or deception

9. NETSNEETM = 9. TENEMENTS
   Apartment houses over-crowded and poorly maintained

10. IESLCELAYP = 10. ESPECIALLY
    To a great degree; very much

11. NROMO = 11. MORON
    Stupid person

12. SOVORIERC = 12. CORROSIVE
    Capable of destroying slowly by chemical action

13. UMLRIAUSOC = 13. MIRACULOUS
    Like a miracle; happening without any natural or scientific explanation

14. ALDYARPZE = 14. PARALYZED
    Caused to be incapable of movement

15. CTPALAURRI = 15. PARTICULAR
    Specific; a certain one

Freak the Mighty Vocabulary Juggle Letters 2

1. NEATIASOMFTIN = 1. _____
   Object that shows or embodies something

2. IBNGAOOLIT = 2. _____
   Duty

3. PEECTVRIPES = 3. _____
   A view or outlook

4. AMPDIRY = 4. _____
   Structure with a square or triangular base and sloping sides that meet in a point at the top

5. TRTRYCAOJE = 5. _____
   The path of a moving body or particle

6. NNAICDSOULTYF = 6. _____
   Not operating normally or properly

7. LMTTEYERE = 7. _____
   Transmission of readings to a distant receiving set or station

8. MREADRSSABE = 8. _____
   To feel self-conscious or ill at ease

9. OVREOISRC = 9. _____
   Capable of destroying slowly by chemical action

10. NIVTINEONTER =10. _____
    Action taken to improve a medical disorder

11. MAOEPRYRT =11. _____
    Not lasting

12. TINFRAC =12. _____
    Conducted in a hurried and chaotic way; full of fear or anxiety

13. RDTUSES =13. _____
    Tied up

14. RIAUCAPLTR =14. _____
    Specific; a certain one

15. YRCEUNG =15. _____
    Need for immediate attention or action

Freak the Mighty Vocabulary Juggle Letters 2 Answer Key

1. NEATIASOMFTIN = 1. MANIFESTATION
   Object that shows or embodies something

2. IBNGAOOLIT = 2. OBLIGATION
   Duty

3. PEECTVRIPES = 3. PERSPECTIVE
   A view or outlook

4. AMPDIRY = 4. PYRAMID
   Structure with a square or triangular base and sloping sides that meet in a point at the top

5. TRTRYCAOJE = 5. TRAJECTORY
   The path of a moving body or particle

6. NNAICDSOULTYF = 6. DYSFUNCTIONAL
   Not operating normally or properly

7. LMTTEYERE = 7. TELEMETRY
   Transmission of readings to a distant receiving set or station

8. MREADRSSABE = 8. EMBARRASSED
   To feel self-conscious or ill at ease

9. OVREOISRC = 9. CORROSIVE
   Capable of destroying slowly by chemical action

10. NIVTINEONTER = 10. INTERVENTION
    Action taken to improve a medical disorder

11. MAOEPRYRT = 11. TEMPORARY
    Not lasting

12. TINFRAC = 12. FRANTIC
    Conducted in a hurried and chaotic way; full of fear or anxiety

13. RDTUSES = 13. TRUSSED
    Tied up

14. RIAUCAPLTR = 14. PARTICULAR
    Specific; a certain one

15. YRCEUNG = 15. URGENCY
    Need for immediate attention or action

Freak the Mighty Vocabulary Juggle Letters 3

1. ROEUPISC = 1. _____
   Valuable; having great value

2. EUNUQI = 2. _____
   One of a kind

3. OSNCIADOMAOCTM = 3. _____
   Living space; lodgings

4. REDSSUT = 4. _____
   Tied up

5. HYONP = 5. _____
   Fake

6. EQSNOCESUNEC = 6. _____
   Results of one's actions

7. DGPYOIR = 7. _____
   Young person with exceptional abilities

8. LTAEYF = 8. _____
   Loyalty; faithfulness

9. IELATVO = 9. _____
   Break or fail to comply with a rule or agreement

10. DLUIGVDE = 10. _____
    Made known; revealed

11. NAOBAIRTER = 11. _____
    Unwelcome deviation from normal

12. UNISCEJTI = 12. _____
    Something unfair and wrong

13. OBIATINLGO = 13. _____
    Duty

14. LPEEX = 14. _____
    Eject forcefully

15. CHPTEYRAE = 15. _____
    An original model

Freak the Mighty Vocabulary Juggle Letters 3 Answer Key

1. ROEUPISC = 1. PRECIOUS
   Valuable; having great value

2. EUNUQI = 2. UNIQUE
   One of a kind

3. OSNCIADOMAOCTM = 3. ACCOMMODATIONS
   Living space; lodgings

4. REDSSUT = 4. TRUSSED
   Tied up

5. HYONP = 5. PHONY
   Fake

6. EQSNOCESUNEC = 6. CONSEQUENCES
   Results of one's actions

7. DGPYOIR = 7. PRODIGY
   Young person with exceptional abilities

8. LTAEYF = 8. FEALTY
   Loyalty; faithfulness

9. IELATVO = 9. VIOLATE
   Break or fail to comply with a rule or agreement

10. DLUIGVDE = 10. DIVULGED
    Made known; revealed

11. NAOBAIRTER = 11. ABERRATION
    Unwelcome deviation from normal

12. UNISCEJTI = 12. INJUSTICE
    Something unfair and wrong

13. OBIATINLGO = 13. OBLIGATION
    Duty

14. LPEEX = 14. EXPEL
    Eject forcefully

15. CHPTEYRAE = 15. ARCHETYPE
    An original model

Freak the Mighty Vocabulary Juggle Letters 4

1. OLHMODU = 1. _____
   Tough and aggressive young man

2. ATOH = 2. _____
   Solemn promise

3. ILNOIOTBGA = 3. _____
   Duty

4. LYFAET = 4. _____
   Loyalty; faithfulness

5. EZRAAYLPD = 5. _____
   Caused to be incapable of movement

6. EESTD = 6. _____
   Horse

7. VSIEEAV = 7. _____
   Tending or intended to avoid

8. IIBASZLDET = 8. _____
   Balanced; made less likely to fall

9. UTNJISCEI = 9. _____
   Something unfair and wrong

10. NNITVOENI =10. _____
    Something newly created

11. GRIUAETGETR =11. _____
    To vomit

12. YAPMIRD =12. _____
    Structure with a square or triangular base and sloping sides that meet in a point at the top

13. CASAITOOCMDMNO =13. _____
    Living space; lodgings

14. QENIUU =14. _____
    One of a kind

15. IEVRATERL =15. _____
    Act or process of getting something back

Freak the Mighty Vocabulary Juggle Letters 4 Answer Key

1. OLHMODU = 1. HOODLUM
   Tough and aggressive young man

2. ATOH = 2. OATH
   Solemn promise

3. ILNOIOTBGA = 3. OBLIGATION
   Duty

4. LYFAET = 4. FEALTY
   Loyalty; faithfulness

5. EZRAAYLPD = 5. PARALYZED
   Caused to be incapable of movement

6. EESTD = 6. STEED
   Horse

7. VSIEEAV = 7. EVASIVE
   Tending or intended to avoid

8. IIBASZLDET = 8. STABILIZED
   Balanced; made less likely to fall

9. UTNJISCEI = 9. INJUSTICE
   Something unfair and wrong

10. NNITVOENI =10. INVENTION
    Something newly created

11. GRIUAETGETR =11. REGURGITATE
    To vomit

12. YAPMIRD =12. PYRAMID
    Structure with a square or triangular base and sloping sides that meet in a point at the top

13. CASAITOOCMDMNO =13. ACCOMMODATIONS
    Living space; lodgings

14. QENIUU =14. UNIQUE
    One of a kind

15. IEVRATERL =15. RETRIEVAL
    Act or process of getting something back

ABDUCT	Take (someone) away illegally by force or deception
ABERRATION	Unwelcome deviation from normal
ACCOMMODATIONS	Living space; lodgings
ALTERNATIVES	Choices
ARCHETYPE	An original model

AUTOMATIC	Working by itself with little or no direct human control
CAMOUFLAGE	Protective coloring or disguise
CONSEQUENCES	Results of one's actions
CONVERGING	Coming together in one place
CORROSIVE	Capable of destroying slowly by chemical action

DELIGHTED	Very happy
DEMEANOR	The way a person behaves
DETENTION	Punishment of being kept in school after hours
DIVULGED	Made known; revealed
DYSFUNCTIONAL	Not operating normally or properly

DYSLEXIC	Having difficulty interpreting words, letters, and symbols
EMBARRASSED	To feel self-conscious or ill at ease
ESPECIALLY	To a great degree; very much
EVASIVE	Tending or intended to avoid
EXPEL	Eject forcefully

EXPRESSION	Word or phrase communicating an idea
FACILITATE	Make easier
FEALTY	Loyalty; faithfulness
FIERCE	Violent or aggressive; ferocious
FRANTIC	Conducted in a hurried and chaotic way; full of fear or anxiety

FUNCTIONAL	Useful; practical; working
FURROWED	Trenched; rutted; grooved; wrinkled
HOODLUM	Tough and aggressive young man
HYPNOTIZED	Put into a trance
IGNORANT	Lacking knowledge

INJUSTICE	Something unfair and wrong
INTENSIVE	Concentrated; thorough
INTERVENTION	Action taken to improve a medical disorder
INVENTION	Something newly created
MANIFESTATION	Object that shows or embodies something

MIRACULOUS	Like a miracle; happening without any natural or scientific explanation
MORON	Stupid person
OATH	Solemn promise
OBLIGATION	Duty
OBNOXIOUS	Extremely unpleasant

OPTIMUM	Most favorable; best
PARALYZED	Caused to be incapable of movement
PARTICULAR	Specific; a certain one
PERSPECTIVE	A view or outlook
PHONY	Fake

POSSESSED	Controlled as if by a spirit or other force
PRECAUTION	Measure taken in advance to prevent something undesirable from happening
PRECIOUS	Valuable; having great value
PRODIGY	Young person with exceptional abilities
PROPULSION	Force that sends forward

PYRAMID	Structure with a square or triangular base and sloping sides that meet in a point at the top
REGURGITATE	To vomit
REMARKABLE	Uncommon; worthy of notice
RETRIEVAL	Act or process of getting something back
RINGER	Informal term for a person's double

SCUTTLE	Run hurriedly with short, quick steps
SOBRIQUET	Nickname
STABILIZED	Balanced; made less likely to fall
STEED	Horse
TELEMETRY	Transmission of readings to a distant receiving set or station

TEMPORARY	Not lasting
TENEMENTS	Apartment houses over-crowded and poorly maintained
TRACHEOTOMY	Incision in the windpipe made to relieve an obstruction to breathing
TRAJECTORY	The path of a moving body or particle
TROUSERS	Pants

TRUSSED	Tied up
UNIQUE	One of a kind
URGENCY	Need for immediate attention or action
VIOLATE	Break or fail to comply with a rule or agreement

Freak the Mighty Vocabulary

STABILIZED	EVASIVE	DYSLEXIC	TRUSSED	DELIGHTED
RETRIEVAL	CAMOUFLAGE	DIVULGED	EXPEL	EXPRESSION
PRECIOUS	ABDUCT	FREE SPACE	DETENTION	URGENCY
VIOLATE	PRECAUTION	STEED	HOODLUM	TEMPORARY
ALTERNATIVES	DEMEANOR	SCUTTLE	PRODIGY	PHONY

Freak the Mighty Vocabulary

INVENTION	EMBARRASSED	OBNOXIOUS	ACCOMMODATIONS	FIERCE
PERSPECTIVE	PROPULSION	PARALYZED	TRAJECTORY	TENEMENTS
HYPNOTIZED	SOBRIQUET	FREE SPACE	RINGER	OPTIMUM
DYSFUNCTIONAL	FURROWED	TROUSERS	CONVERGING	MIRACULOUS
MORON	TRACHEOTOMY	FACILITATE	FEALTY	MANIFESTATION

Freak the Mighty Vocabulary

SCUTTLE	TROUSERS	TRACHEOTOMY	FACILITATE	URGENCY
INTERVENTION	DYSLEXIC	PYRAMID	PRECAUTION	HOODLUM
EVASIVE	DELIGHTED	FREE SPACE	INJUSTICE	TEMPORARY
DETENTION	OBLIGATION	STEED	ALTERNATIVES	ABERRATION
PHONY	MIRACULOUS	OATH	HYPNOTIZED	FUNCTIONAL

Freak the Mighty Vocabulary

STABILIZED	OBNOXIOUS	PERSPECTIVE	CONVERGING	OPTIMUM
CONSEQUENCES	AUTOMATIC	FURROWED	MANIFESTATION	INVENTION
DIVULGED	TELEMETRY	FREE SPACE	REMARKABLE	DYSFUNCTIONAL
FEALTY	MORON	FIERCE	PARTICULAR	CORROSIVE
TRUSSED	FRANTIC	SOBRIQUET	ACCOMMODATIONS	UNIQUE

Freak the Mighty Vocabulary

IGNORANT	SOBRIQUET	RINGER	ABDUCT	EVASIVE
TRUSSED	INVENTION	SCUTTLE	OPTIMUM	PRODIGY
OATH	REMARKABLE	FREE SPACE	PYRAMID	DELIGHTED
VIOLATE	HYPNOTIZED	ABERRATION	URGENCY	TRACHEOTOMY
UNIQUE	TEMPORARY	HOODLUM	INJUSTICE	CONVERGING

Freak the Mighty Vocabulary

FEALTY	FACILITATE	PROPULSION	ALTERNATIVES	OBNOXIOUS
PERSPECTIVE	EXPEL	MIRACULOUS	EMBARRASSED	ACCOMMODATIONS
INTENSIVE	CONSEQUENCES	FREE SPACE	POSSESSED	STEED
OBLIGATION	MORON	DETENTION	TROUSERS	TENEMENTS
TELEMETRY	STABILIZED	FUNCTIONAL	FIERCE	ESPECIALLY

Freak the Mighty Vocabulary

DYSLEXIC	FIERCE	EMBARRASSED	INJUSTICE	PRECIOUS
TRAJECTORY	TRUSSED	RETRIEVAL	EVASIVE	REGURGITATE
PRECAUTION	STABILIZED	FREE SPACE	MORON	OBNOXIOUS
EXPRESSION	FRANTIC	OATH	FURROWED	DETENTION
PARTICULAR	ABERRATION	HYPNOTIZED	ACCOMMODATIONS	REMARKABLE

Freak the Mighty Vocabulary

PYRAMID	TROUSERS	TRACHEOTOMY	MIRACULOUS	ABDUCT
CONVERGING	PHONY	VIOLATE	OPTIMUM	HOODLUM
INTERVENTION	POSSESSED	FREE SPACE	PARALYZED	PERSPECTIVE
SOBRIQUET	DIVULGED	FEALTY	UNIQUE	TELEMETRY
ARCHETYPE	RINGER	TENEMENTS	FACILITATE	CAMOUFLAGE

Freak the Mighty Vocabulary

URGENCY	FRANTIC	RETRIEVAL	DELIGHTED	CONSEQUENCES
SCUTTLE	PRECIOUS	PRECAUTION	UNIQUE	HYPNOTIZED
INTENSIVE	MORON	FREE SPACE	CAMOUFLAGE	OATH
RINGER	EMBARRASSED	TRAJECTORY	INTERVENTION	FUNCTIONAL
VIOLATE	FIERCE	AUTOMATIC	STABILIZED	ALTERNATIVES

Freak the Mighty Vocabulary

FACILITATE	MIRACULOUS	CORROSIVE	DYSFUNCTIONAL	ABDUCT
TROUSERS	DYSLEXIC	SOBRIQUET	EXPRESSION	INVENTION
PARTICULAR	TENEMENTS	FREE SPACE	ABERRATION	TRUSSED
IGNORANT	ESPECIALLY	REMARKABLE	EVASIVE	INJUSTICE
PHONY	PARALYZED	HOODLUM	DETENTION	FURROWED

Freak the Mighty Vocabulary

ALTERNATIVES	URGENCY	DYSLEXIC	INTENSIVE	ESPECIALLY
IGNORANT	OBNOXIOUS	CONSEQUENCES	PYRAMID	UNIQUE
ABDUCT	TEMPORARY	FREE SPACE	MORON	MANIFESTATION
SCUTTLE	PARTICULAR	ACCOMMODATIONS	FEALTY	ARCHETYPE
PROPULSION	TROUSERS	RECURCITATE	PHONY	REMARKABLE

Freak the Mighty Vocabulary

OPTIMUM	POSSESSED	DYSFUNCTIONAL	VIOLATE	CAMOUFLAGE
EXPRESSION	ABERRATION	HOODLUM	EMBARRASSED	RINGER
RETRIEVAL	DEMEANOR	FREE SPACE	FUNCTIONAL	PRECAUTION
PERSPECTIVE	TRUSSED	DETENTION	AUTOMATIC	STABILIZED
TRACHEOTOMY	FACILITATE	OBLIGATION	DIVULGED	EXPEL

Freak the Mighty Vocabulary

PHONY	AUTOMATIC	PRODIGY	DIVULGED	PARTICULAR
ARCHETYPE	FACILITATE	PYRAMID	POSSESSED	OBNOXIOUS
DYSFUNCTIONAL	STABILIZED	FREE SPACE	UNIQUE	DEMEANOR
VIOLATE	CORROSIVE	DETENTION	INJUSTICE	REMARKABLE
TRUSSED	ACCOMMODATIONS	ABDUCT	SCUTTLE	TROUSERS

Freak the Mighty Vocabulary

CONVERGING	PRECAUTION	ABERRATION	MORON	FURROWED
CONSEQUENCES	PERSPECTIVE	INVENTION	DYSLEXIC	FIERCE
OBLIGATION	INTENSIVE	FREE SPACE	MANIFESTATION	EMBARRASSED
REGURGITATE	HYPNOTIZED	INTERVENTION	EVASIVE	SOBRIQUET
FUNCTIONAL	TRACHEOTOMY	FRANTIC	PROPULSION	STEED

Freak the Mighty Vocabulary

REGURGITATE	PHONY	INJUSTICE	SCUTTLE	PYRAMID
ABERRATION	DELIGHTED	EXPRESSION	CAMOUFLAGE	TROUSERS
FRANTIC	MANIFESTATION	FREE SPACE	ABDUCT	ACCOMMODATIONS
UNIQUE	DYSFUNCTIONAL	CONSEQUENCES	STABILIZED	HYPNOTIZED
ESPECIALLY	AUTOMATIC	DIVULGED	MIRACULOUS	ALTERNATIVES

Freak the Mighty Vocabulary

HOODLUM	TRACHEOTOMY	RETRIEVAL	FURROWED	INTERVENTION
EVASIVE	PRECIOUS	OPTIMUM	INTENSIVE	STEED
PARTICULAR	URGENCY	FREE SPACE	POSSESSED	VIOLATE
EXPEL	EMBARRASSED	TRAJECTORY	TRUSSED	TEMPORARY
DYSLEXIC	OBNOXIOUS	FEALTY	IGNORANT	PARALYZED

Freak the Mighty Vocabulary

REMARKABLE	PHONY	ABDUCT	TRAJECTORY	FIERCE
ESPECIALLY	FEALTY	CONSEQUENCES	OPTIMUM	MORON
CAMOUFLAGE	TENEMENTS	FREE SPACE	DIVULGED	DETENTION
MANIFESTATION	PRECIOUS	URGENCY	DYSLEXIC	CONVERGING
TELEMETRY	PRECAUTION	IGNORANT	POSSESSED	STABILIZED

Freak the Mighty Vocabulary

PRODIGY	HOODLUM	RINGER	PYRAMID	PARTICULAR
TRUSSED	DEMEANOR	EMBARRASSED	SCUTTLE	UNIQUE
FRANTIC	FURROWED	FREE SPACE	HYPNOTIZED	ARCHETYPE
SOBRIQUET	INTERVENTION	STEED	MIRACULOUS	ACCOMMODATIONS
DELIGHTED	TRACHEOTOMY	ALTERNATIVES	PERSPECTIVE	TEMPORARY

Freak the Mighty Vocabulary

INJUSTICE	EVASIVE	CONVERGING	PHONY	IGNORANT
SCUTTLE	OBLIGATION	TELEMETRY	ABERRATION	INVENTION
EMBARRASSED	CORROSIVE	FREE SPACE	RETRIEVAL	PROPULSION
FIERCE	FUNCTIONAL	ACCOMMODATIONS	EXPEL	REMARKABLE
ALTERNATIVES	REGURGITATE	MIRACULOUS	FURROWED	URGENCY

Freak the Mighty Vocabulary

DYSLEXIC	DEMEANOR	TRAJECTORY	HYPNOTIZED	TENEMENTS
TRUSSED	EXPRESSION	UNIQUE	PRECIOUS	FEALTY
DETENTION	OPTIMUM	FREE SPACE	FRANTIC	ESPECIALLY
PERSPECTIVE	TEMPORARY	INTERVENTION	MANIFESTATION	POSSESSED
STEED	INTENSIVE	AUTOMATIC	FACILITATE	OBNOXIOUS

Freak the Mighty Vocabulary

FIERCE	PHONY	DYSFUNCTIONAL	TEMPORARY	HOODLUM
INTENSIVE	PARALYZED	REGURGITATE	OPTIMUM	OBNOXIOUS
ACCOMMODATIONS	EVASIVE	FREE SPACE	PERSPECTIVE	HYPNOTIZED
AUTOMATIC	TRACHEOTOMY	RINGER	REMARKABLE	VIOLATE
CONVERGING	FUNCTIONAL	CORROSIVE	STEED	ABDUCT

Freak the Mighty Vocabulary

SOBRIQUET	FURROWED	ALTERNATIVES	CONSEQUENCES	TROUSERS
INTERVENTION	IGNORANT	PYRAMID	INJUSTICE	ARCHETYPE
UNIQUE	PRECIOUS	FREE SPACE	FACILITATE	MORON
ABERRATION	SCUTTLE	TRAJECTORY	MIRACULOUS	DELIGHTED
RETRIEVAL	FEALTY	MANIFESTATION	PRODIGY	EMBARRASSED

Freak the Mighty Vocabulary

ESPECIALLY	ALTERNATIVES	OATH	TROUSERS	PHONY
MANIFESTATION	EXPRESSION	HYPNOTIZED	OBLIGATION	TRAJECTORY
POSSESSED	RINGER	FREE SPACE	INTENSIVE	EVASIVE
IGNORANT	ARCHETYPE	OBNOXIOUS	FACILITATE	STABILIZED
REMARKABLE	DYSLEXIC	FRANTIC	REGURGITATE	FIERCE

Freak the Mighty Vocabulary

ABERRATION	EMBARRASSED	CONSEQUENCES	AUTOMATIC	PARTICULAR
CONVERGING	RETRIEVAL	VIOLATE	TELEMETRY	OPTIMUM
SCUTTLE	INVENTION	FREE SPACE	UNIQUE	INTERVENTION
SOBRIQUET	PROPULSION	MORON	PARALYZED	DELIGHTED
FUNCTIONAL	EXPEL	STEED	DETENTION	DEMEANOR

Freak the Mighty Vocabulary

HOODLUM	TELEMETRY	REGURGITATE	DYSFUNCTIONAL	ACCOMMODATIONS
OPTIMUM	ALTERNATIVES	UNIQUE	AUTOMATIC	TROUSERS
DETENTION	EMBARRASSED	FREE SPACE	CAMOUFLAGE	EXPEL
PRECAUTION	ABERRATION	POSSESSED	MANIFESTATION	TEMPORARY
FEALTY	CORROSIVE	STABILIZED	TRUSSED	FURROWED

Freak the Mighty Vocabulary

HYPNOTIZED	PYRAMID	DYSLEXIC	URGENCY	FUNCTIONAL
FIERCE	PARTICULAR	ARCHETYPE	MIRACULOUS	PHONY
INTENSIVE	FRANTIC	FREE SPACE	TENEMENTS	RINGER
IGNORANT	PRODIGY	FACILITATE	DIVULGED	TRAJECTORY
RETRIEVAL	DEMEANOR	CONSEQUENCES	PROPULSION	PARALYZED

Freak the Mighty Vocabulary

PARTICULAR	TRUSSED	HYPNOTIZED	PHONY	ALTERNATIVES
ACCOMMODATIONS	EMBARRASSED	URGENCY	DELIGHTED	INJUSTICE
FIERCE	MORON	FREE SPACE	SCUTTLE	REGURGITATE
FRANTIC	TENEMENTS	DEMEANOR	INTENSIVE	TELEMETRY
FEALTY	INTERVENTION	DIVULGED	CAMOUFLAGE	RETRIEVAL

Freak the Mighty Vocabulary

UNIQUE	OBNOXIOUS	TEMPORARY	CONSEQUENCES	HOODLUM
ABERRATION	PYRAMID	TRAJECTORY	IGNORANT	FACILITATE
ESPECIALLY	INVENTION	FREE SPACE	STEED	TRACHEOTOMY
MANIFESTATION	ARCHETYPE	FURROWED	OATH	OPTIMUM
REMARKABLE	ABDUCT	PARALYZED	OBLIGATION	VIOLATE

Freak the Mighty Vocabulary

SOBRIQUET	ABERRATION	ALTERNATIVES	PYRAMID	DELIGHTED
OATH	TRACHEOTOMY	TRAJECTORY	EXPRESSION	AUTOMATIC
EMBARRASSED	VIOLATE	FREE SPACE	TROUSERS	ACCOMMODATIONS
ARCHETYPE	TENEMENTS	INJUSTICE	DIVULGED	ESPECIALLY
DYSLEXIC	PRODIGY	SCUTTLE	INTENSIVE	REGURGITATE

Freak the Mighty Vocabulary

PHONY	URGENCY	PARTICULAR	TEMPORARY	FACILITATE
CORROSIVE	STABILIZED	PROPULSION	CAMOUFLAGE	PRECIOUS
EVASIVE	IGNORANT	FREE SPACE	POSSESSED	PARALYZED
STEED	OBLIGATION	HOODLUM	ABDUCT	HYPNOTIZED
MORON	FIERCE	FURROWED	INTERVENTION	OPTIMUM

Freak the Mighty Vocabulary

EVASIVE	EMBARRASSED	FURROWED	DETENTION	OPTIMUM
INTERVENTION	INTENSIVE	URGENCY	PYRAMID	HOODLUM
PRECIOUS	FRANTIC	FREE SPACE	PROPULSION	FEALTY
DYSFUNCTIONAL	CORROSIVE	DELIGHTED	STEED	FACILITATE
RINGER	EXPEL	PARTICULAR	FIERCE	VIOLATE

Freak the Mighty Vocabulary

PARALYZED	TENEMENTS	REMARKABLE	TRUSSED	PRECAUTION
CONVERGING	TRACHEOTOMY	MORON	MIRACULOUS	TEMPORARY
DEMEANOR	ABERRATION	FREE SPACE	RETRIEVAL	ACCOMMODATIONS
OBLIGATION	POSSESSED	CONSEQUENCES	ESPECIALLY	PRODIGY
REGURGITATE	MANIFESTATION	AUTOMATIC	TRAJECTORY	INJUSTICE

www.ingramcontent.com/pod-product-compliance
Lightning Source LLC
Chambersburg PA
CBHW081452070526
44586CB00019B/2323